PACIFIC VOICES

PACIFIC VOICES

KEEPING OUR CULTURES ALIVE

MIRIAM KAHN and ERIN YOUNGER

with photographs by MARY RANDLETT and SAM VAN FLEET

UNIVERSITY OF WASHINGTON PRESS | SEATTLE AND LONDON

IN ASSOCIATION WITH

BURKE MUSEUM OF NATURAL HISTORY AND CULTURE | SEATTLE

Publication of this book is supported by a generous grant from the Geneva Foundation.

Copyright © 2005 by University of Washington Press

Printed in China

10 09 08 07 06 05   5 4 3 2 1

Designed by Ashley Saleeba

Map by Barry Levely

UNIVERSITY OF WASHINGTON PRESS

P.O. Box 50096, Seattle, WA 98145, U.S.A.

www.washington.edu/uwpress

The paper used in this publication meets the minimum requirements of American National Standard for Information Sciences—Permanence of Paper for Printed Library Materials, ANSI Z39.48-1984.♾

Library of Congress Cataloging-in-Publication Data

Pacific voices : keeping our cultures alive / [edited by] Miriam Kahn and Erin Younger ; photographs by Mary Randlett and Sam Van Fleet.

  p. cm.

"Book springs from 'Pacific Voices', a longterm exhibit that opened at the Burke Museum in late 1997"—Ack.

Includes bibliographical references and index.

ISBN 0-295-98550-x (pbk. : alk. paper)

 1. Material culture—Washington (State)—Exhibitions. 2. Material culture—Asia—Exhibitions. 3. Material culture—Oceania—Exhibitions. 4. Indians of North America—Material culture—Exhibitions. 5. Pacific Islanders—Material culture—Exhibitions. 6. Asians—Material culture—Exhibitions. 7. Burke Museum of Natural History and Culture—Exhibitions. I. Kahn, Miriam. II. Younger, Erin. III. Burke Museum of Natural History and Culture.

GN560.U6P33 2005

306'.074'797772—dc22

2005013311

Frontispiece:
Nicole Shimizu at Obon, Seattle, 1998. *Photograph by Richard L. Taylor.*

We would like to acknowledge with gratitude two servant leadership

organizations dedicated to developing community leaders:

THE NORTHWEST ASSOCIATION OF PACIFIC AMERICANS (NAPA) *and*

THE NATIONAL PACIFIC AMERICAN LEADERSHIP INSTITUTE (NAPALI)

CONTENTS

ACKNOWLEDGMENTS

THE GENESIS OF THIS BOOK SPRINGS from "Pacific Voices," a long-term exhibit that opened at the Burke Museum in late 1997. Many individuals involved in the planning and production of the exhibit, as well as others who joined them later, contributed to the creation of this publication. To all, we offer our warmest, heartfelt thanks. Following are some specific acknowledgments.

The numerous contributors whose voices are highlighted in the book shared generously of their memories and stories, proofread their chapters, searched through family albums for photographs, and gave abundantly of their time and energy in their otherwise busy lives.

Northwest photographer Mary Randlett took the formal portraits of the contributors; Sam Van Fleet photographed the main object in each chapter and documented several related events.

Other photographers, illustrators, and artists granted permission to reproduce their images: James Cooper Abbott, William Alkire, Anthony Fitiafiafi Barber, Jerry Lynne Barber, Veronica Leasiolagi Barber, Brian Brake, David Brown, Jack Buzzard, Min-chih Chou, Rose Dang, Paula Chandler David, Natalie B. Fobes, Lauren Greenfield, David Hawelmai, Bill Hess, Vi Hilbert, Lowell D. Holmes, Karl Hutterer, Moodette Ka'apana, Miriam Kahn, Herb Kawainui Kane, Kauanoe, Edwin B. Kayton, Edward B. Liebow, Sarah Loudon, Chana Meddin, Ron Peltier, Songsak Prangwatthanakun, Su Ratsamee, Richard L. Taylor, and Stephen Thomas.

Various photographic collections, museums, archives, and presses also granted use rights: Auckland Art Gallery Toi o Tāmaki, Bess Press, Bishop Museum, Burke Museum, Calderdale Museums and Arts, Lummi Archives, *Mana* magazine, Matson Navigation Company, National Library of New Zealand / Te Puna

Matauranga o Aotearoa, New Zealand Te Papa Tongarewa, Royal British Columbia Museum, University of Auckland Department of Maori Studies and Anthropology, University of Washington Library Special Collections Division, and Wing Luke Asian Museum.

Sam Yum assisted with photo research, manuscript preparation, and the development of supplementary materials for use with the book in schools. Washington Middle School teacher Richard Katz helped with the conceptualization of the school materials.

Susan Hayes-McQueen assisted with the interviews and transcribed many hours of tape. Ben Cruz, Shaine Ganz, Nicole Nathan, and Shara Svendsen assisted during the early phases of research and photography.

The Dean's Office and the Royalty Research Fund of the University of Washington, the Sidney Fund, Nancy Skinner Nordhoff, King County 4 Culture, and the Port of Seattle contributed generous financial support at various stages of this project, including support for research, photography, photographic rights and use fees, and publication.

The Geneva Foundation of Edmonds, Washington, made an extremely generous donation to the University of Washington Press, which not only made publication possible but ensured that the book's price would be affordable for the general public, schools, and libraries.

The University of Washington Press staff, especially director J. Pat Soden, editorial manager Marilyn Trueblood, copyeditor Kerrie Maynes, and designer Ashley Saleeba, were patient and encouraging in their work with us and helped make this long-term dream a reality.

PACIFIC VOICES

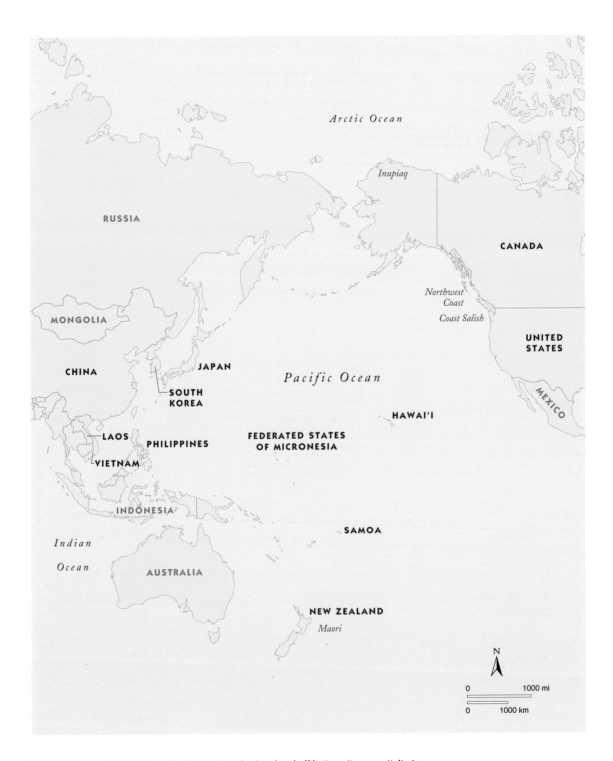

Pacific Voices contributors' homelands (in red) and cultural and affiliations (in green italics).

INTRODUCTION

The Objects of Culture

MIRIAM KAHN

THIS BOOK IS ABOUT THE VIBRANT connections between objects, people, and cultural identity. In exploring these links, each chapter brings an object to life through personal stories—stories of change and loss, memories and endurance, revival and pride. Readers will become acquainted with the many narrators and with how, when confronting change, each holds on to an identity that is, after all, resilient and pliant and always a creative mix of cultural traditions and personal experiences.

Everywhere in the world, people use technical skill and creative vision to transform raw materials into objects that are useful, often meaningful, and sometimes beautiful. Objects in part help people define who they are, connect to their past, and share their values. For example, an elegant Maori (MAOW-ree) feather cloak from New Zealand proudly draped over the shoulders of an elderly woman indicates her elevated status. As a Maori woman explained, those Maori who see her wearing the cloak, whether in New Zealand or the United States, know that she has "earned her respect because she has gone through life serving other people." A Nuu-chah-nulth (NOO-CHAH-noolth) wolf headdress is, as its carver explains, "who we are, our power, our identity." When the carver looks at the headdress he hears the voice of the wolf, who is with him whether he is in his forested homeland on the west coast of Vancouver Island or in an apartment in an American city. An unadorned bamboo wind instrument from Laos brings back memories that are both painful and comforting to Lao emigrants to the United States who listen to its melodious sounds in their new environment. As he listens, one man closes his eyes, thinks of his lost homeland to which the music temporarily transports him, and feels "like a drop on the floor."

Objects—like the lives of the people who make and use them—are constantly changing and adapting. People come up with new ideas for the raw materials that they fashion into objects. Today, when making a cloak, the Maori artist might pluck the feathers she will use from an imported Chinese feather duster rather than from a New Zealand chicken. Artists also adapt the styles in which they work. When carving a wolf headdress, a Northwest Coast artist receives inspiration from museum collections, photographs, and books as well as from fellow artists. Even though he has created more than thirty headdresses, each time "there's always that push, that twist, to make it a little different." While carving, he tries to stay within, but also to move beyond, the boundaries of cultural tradition. People also carry objects across borders, find new homes for them, and use them in new ways. Lao refugees have transported bamboo wind instruments across oceans, cradling them by hand at airport baggage checkpoints to assure their safety. By understanding the ongoing transformations of objects—in the materials used, the styles followed, and the uses to which they are put—we gain access to rich lessons in cultural history that can help us better understand the vitality and cultural adaptability of our complex world.

Today, the human landscape is changing more rapidly than ever before, as people from all over the world cross political and cultural borders and move in and out of multiple cultural contexts. Some people spend their lives weaving back and forth between cultures, doing so as often and as effortlessly as they step onto an airplane. Others, such as Native Americans, have not had to move far to experience major changes and massive disruptions in their lives. Whether moving across borders or settled in one place, people today live in a world of multicultural experiences, a reality made even more commonplace and bewildering by the existence of videos, the Internet, and cell phones.

Precisely because our world can be one of dizzying movement and change, sources of stability seem more important than ever. When parents and children speak different languages, prefer different foods, wear different clothing, and adhere to different values, how do individuals maintain their cultural identity and know who they are? As one of the *taiko* (TYE-koh) drummers interviewed for this book asked, "In the melting pot of the United States, how do you hold on to your heritage? How do you hold on to who you are?"

It is precisely at times of disruption and displacement that objects can take on added meaning. Objects can serve as emotional anchors in a sea of change. They can take on new roles for people wanting to learn or teach about their cultural heritage. They can help us understand how people continually sustain and affirm their cultural identity. Human beings have an amazing ability to create a sense of stability and integration in the face of chaos and fragmentation, working with the various threads of cultural traditions they have at their disposal.

The United States is more culturally diverse than any other country in the world. Its native inhabitants have been met by unending waves of immigrants, the first of which arrived over 500 years ago. These immigrants, while bringing radical and sometimes destructive changes, have also experienced their own cultural dislocation and loss by having to leave something of themselves behind. Yet almost everyone, everywhere, manages to hang on to something of their past and adapt it to their new life. The "something" may be a language, a dance, a ceremony, knowledge, values, or physical things—"the objects of culture." These objects may be used in their original form or created anew from fragments and memories of the past. Whether treasured from long ago or fashioned anew, each has its own story.

The stories in this book were collected in tandem with the "Pacific Voices" exhibit that opened at the Burke Museum in Seattle, Washington, in 1997. During the exhibit's planning and installation, museum staff worked closely with over one hundred community advisors from Seattle's Pacific Islander, Southeast Asian, East Asian, and Northwest Native American communities. These advisors wanted the exhibit to explore sources of cultural identity for peoples of the Pacific Rim who now live in the greater Seattle area. They accomplished this through displays of objects that highlighted the personal experiences of various groups.

The most important message the advisors wanted to communicate through the exhibit was that their cultures are very much alive—they wanted the exhibit to sing with life. In order that it might do so, they enriched the objects with personal stories, which, in vastly shortened form,

appeared in label texts and photo captions, and were narrated on video screens throughout the gallery. However, museum interpretive techniques are limited in their ability to convey the depth and richness of people's stories.

Thus, the idea for this book was born. In life, objects are intricately linked to personal experiences, social relations, and cultural roots, as these narratives convey. In writing this book, we worked primarily, although not exclusively, with the same key advisors who had helped with the exhibit. We returned to them and asked each one the same question: "If you could choose one object that represents the richness of your culture and provides you with a sense of cultural identity, what would it be?" We listened to their answers, recorded their stories, and edited them into narratives, adding sidebars to provide contextual information for readers.

We now offer their stories to you. It is our hope that you will be captivated by the depth of knowledge and meaning associated with what, at first glance, may seem like an array of unrelated objects. We also hope that the stories—all from people whose homelands lie along the Pacific Rim—will stimulate your thoughts and memories about your own heritage and sources of cultural identity.

1 HAWAIIAN *PAHU*

Voice of the Gods

'IWALANI CHRISTIAN

"Of all the hula instruments, the pahu *is the most revered. This is because the* pahu *is considered to be the voice of the gods. The drum opening, called* waha, *or mouth, is said to speak."* —'IWALANI CHRISTIAN

Hula *pahu*

The hula *pahu* (PAH-hoo) evolved from the *pahu heiau* (PAH-hoo HAY-yow), or temple drum. In the temple, it was used mostly to call the gods down to be present at ritual ceremonies to guide the priests. Some of the temple rituals had choreographed movements that the priest went through with the beating of the *pahu*. The *pahu* really didn't get utilized for hula until the early 1800s, when the Hawaiian religion was cast

Opposite:
Pahu. *Photograph © 1999 Sam Van Fleet.*

'Iwalani Christian. *Photograph © 2000 Mary Randlett.*

Hula never disappeared: hula dancers with an *ipu* and a *pahu*, ca. 1880s. *Bishop Museum.*

out due to missionary influence. At that time, it came out of the temple and was used as an accompaniment for hula.

Early training in Hawai'i

We lived up in our homestead above Wailua (wye-LOO-ah) Falls on Kaua'i (kau-WYE-ee). We also had a beach residence in Ha'ena (HAH-EH-nah), at the end of the road. On the property where our beach house was, there lived an elderly hula master, Kila Pa. I remember run-ning around as a small child (in the '50s), from our house to the beach, which wasn't very far, and old man Kila Pa would always be out on the porch chanting and drumming. He was trans-ported. Looking back now, I think it was very difficult for him to be in that changing world. The Western and Hawaiian traditions were at terrible battle within him, so he hid himself in his chanting, and he used the *pahu* a lot.

The *pahu* came into my life when I was three or four years old. I received my Hawaiian training through my grandmother, my father's mother. She raised me on the island of Kaua'i. She's the one who helped me embark on my life's voyage. In the Hawaiian tradition, physical signs at your birth tell the elders what your destiny is. I think there were several physical markings that my grandmother saw that made her ask for me; it was common that an elder would ask for a child, and of course refusal was not even considered. This practice, *hanai* (hah-NYE), or *punahele* (POO-nah-HEH-leh), which means "chosen child," is still being carried on now. I think today Hawaiians are trying to recover some of that because they see the importance of keeping the culture alive.

Even though my grandmother was not a hula master, she was groomed in maintaining the family's oral traditions. She had a *pahu* and she began to have me memorize some of these traditions, sometimes accompanying me with her *pahu*. That was the only instrument she had and used, other than clapping with her hands. That continued until I was about eleven, when I really started my hula training. Prior to that, the training was mainly chanting the oral traditions and memorizing. Of course, at that age you don't understand why it's so important to carry on your family's oral traditions, especially when your brothers and sisters don't have to be bur-

dened with that. Even though my parents and my grandparents lived very close together and we spent a lot of time together, I was still under the tutelage and the roof of my grandmother.

When I was growing up, the traditional hula was defunct, and so the traditional instruments were not used in a way that was visible to a lot of people, especially since the tourist industry was at a high upswing. Most of the hula you saw was diluted into the form that is now called "tourist" hula. I was fortunate that I grew up in a situation where traditional hula was still very much alive in my everyday life. But I was also embarrassed, because no one else did that. Very, very few, it seemed, were groomed as I was, so I felt different and embarrassed.

I think I went through several stages, knowing that I couldn't refuse my grandmother or my destiny. My grandmother left us when I was seventeen, while I was still pretty young and searching for my place in the world. But I knew that I had a responsibility; that was something she implanted in me. But I was confused about how far I was going to go with that responsibility. The avenue I took was with hula.

❀ PERSEVERANCE OF HULA ❀

The Hawaiian Islands remained unknown to non-Polynesians until the 1778 voyage of James Cook. Calvinist missionaries arrived in 1820 and discouraged hula, which they thought was frivolous, heathen, and overly sensual. Attacks on hula were supported by those Hawaiian chiefs who had fully converted to Christianity. Hula, however, never disappeared. Hula schools were begun around the islands, and, in the 1860s, chiefs reverted to the custom of having hula performers available to provide entertainment. During the reign of Kalakaua (1871–1891), hula performance became public again. During the early 1900s, when the Hawaiian language was banned in school and at work, hula became a way of keeping the language alive. By the mid-1900s, it was flourishing.

Audiences responded positively to innovations such as music becoming more melodic and dancers placing a greater emphasis on movement. Yet, some of the hula performed has been distorted by those catering to the tourist trade (what Hawaiians call "Hollywood" or "tourist" hula) and has little to do with its traditional roots.

Moving to Seattle

It was my family that brought me to Seattle. My parents moved when I finished high school, so it was a natural move for me, since my grandmother was now gone, to further my education. Our family moved to Seattle because my father had a sister who was here, so he felt comfortable. He had also been looking for better opportunities for the rest of his large family. We have a lot of children. So we moved and I went to school. People saw that I was Hawaiian, and, of course, the first thing they asked was, "Do you sing and dance?" So I started teaching hula in response to people saying, "Oh, I'd like to learn a hula." I really didn't think of starting a *halau* (hah-LAU), or hula studio. It was a difficult time for me as a Hawaiian. I had the chance to be Western and more affluent, in education and material things. Being on the mainland gave me that opportunity. That was what my father wanted for his family—an education, so that we could become better educated than some of the poor families that we grew up around, who didn't have those opportunities. It was as though things Hawaiian were pulling me back, and things Western were making me go ahead.

It was a few years later that I made that transition. When I started teaching, I first taught

When the *pahu* sounds and the sacred songs are chanted, precise movements and expressions are demanded of the dancers. The teacher (*kumu*) directs the dancers through movements for the sacred chants of the hula *pahu*.
Photographs © 1998 Sam Van Fleet.

❀ POETIC CHANTS ❀

Hula is based on poetic chants. It is through such chants that Hawaiians, for generations, have passed on their genealogies, history, religious beliefs, navigation skills, and other aspects of their culture. For example, from early on, there were chants to relate family histories and accounts of the chiefs and gods; to honor warriors; to describe the beauty of a place; to celebrate an important journey; to select and cut a tree to make a canoe; and to teach how to read the wind, waves, and stars. Later, movements were added to illustrate the chants. Some motions depict specific words, such as flowers or birds, while others refer to hidden meanings. Different instruments accompany different kinds of chants and dances. Knowledgeable audience members watch attentively to see how skillfully the hula artists portray the text. Each *kumu hula* (koo-moo HOO-lah) (teacher, director, and choreographer of the performing group) has an individual style and approach.

Chanter. *Print © 1984 by Edwin B. Kayton.*

tourist hula and didn't include the culture that much. The turnaround came when I was in my early twenties. I said, "Oh, my, look at how our people are being portrayed. I know enough to make a difference, and to make sure that the truth is searched out." And that's when I turned over that leaf. My *halau* went from being called "The Hula Hut" to "Na Lei O Manu'akepa" (NAH LAY o mah-noo-ah-KEH-pah). I made that transition from the English language to the Hawaiian language, and the importance of Hawaiian traditions came around too. But I think you have to make that choice. You have to go through that personal transition.

Learning to make a *pahu*

There are several levels of hula training that you go through. In the first level you become a dancer—hula *'olapa* (OH-lah-pah). Next, you become a dance leader—*alaka'i* (ah-lah-kah-EE). Last, you earn your chanter status—*ho'opa'a* (hoh-oh-PAH-ah). Since my chanting started early, I was able to climb into that pretty rapidly and was probably fourteen when I gained *ho'opa'a* status.

Although the *pahu* is the most revered instrument, it is only one of many used for the hula. There are other drums, such as the gourd drum (*ipu heke 'ole*) (EE-POO HEH-keh OH-leh) and double-gourd drum (*ipu heke*) (EE-POO HEH-keh), both made from large hollowed gourds. They are played by beating them with one's hand and tapping them against the ground to produce a "boom-swish-swish" sound. Another type of drum is a small knee drum (*puniu*) (poo-NEE-yoo) that is lashed to one's leg and beaten with a small braided striker. There are bamboo pipes (*ka 'eke 'eke*) (kah EH-keh EH-keh) that are held, one in each hand, and played by striking their open end against a flat rock. Split bamboo rattles (*pu'ili*) (poo-EE-lee) are made of sections of bamboo into which long slits have been cut at one end, from which alternate strips have been removed. They are thought to sound like wind in the trees. Hula sticks of various lengths are made from branches and are played by striking them together. Coconut shell castanets (*niu*) (NEE-yoo), when clicked together, represent the ocean. Stone castanets (*'ili 'ili*) (EE-lee EE-lee) are most valued if they come from the south side of the island of Hawai'i, where, according to legend, the stones give birth to other stones.

One of the requirements, of course, was that I make all my instruments. You start with really simple instruments. It's like earning your right to get to higher phases. The *pahu* is the final instrument you make. Because it's the most revered, it's an important symbol at the time of your graduation exercises: when you enter the area where your graduation exercises are being held, if your *pahu* is sitting on top of the platform, it means that you graduated. But if it's sitting on the floor, you don't go any further into the room. In making my *pahu*, my biggest fear, of course, was that it wouldn't be sitting up on the platform.

When you learn, you're taught what to do, and then you're on your own. The Hawaiian way of teaching is to observe and then go and do it yourself. This is unlike the Western method of asking questions and getting answers. Our teacher taught by making a *pahu*. Later on, of course, if you're training, then you have to make your own, so you have to remember. I'm sure if I had a student now the questions would come, but if there were too many questions, then I would say, "Perhaps you're not ready. You have too many questions. You didn't pay attention."

You can make a *pahu* out of any type of wood. They're made out of breadfruit, coconut, or koa (KOH-ah). I'd like to try to make one out of cedar. I've seen one made out of cedar, where stakes of cedar were made into the drum barrel. It was really interesting. If I'm not mistaken, the Bishop Museum in Honolulu has one that is made from a cedar log that floated to Hawai'i from the Northwest coast of the U.S. mainland. For my first drum, I had an uncle who helped me with the selection of a coconut tree. It had to be one that had been lying for a long time, drying. It was quite a search to find it.

Then I had to decide on my design. The design, of course, is functional because it holds the *'aha* (AH-ha), or the lashing. I decided to do the *hoaka* (HOH-ah-kah), or crescent design. I did two rows, using wood-carving tools. I had planned to do three, but it's awfully hard. *Hoaka* means "to show a shadow" or "to fall upon," and

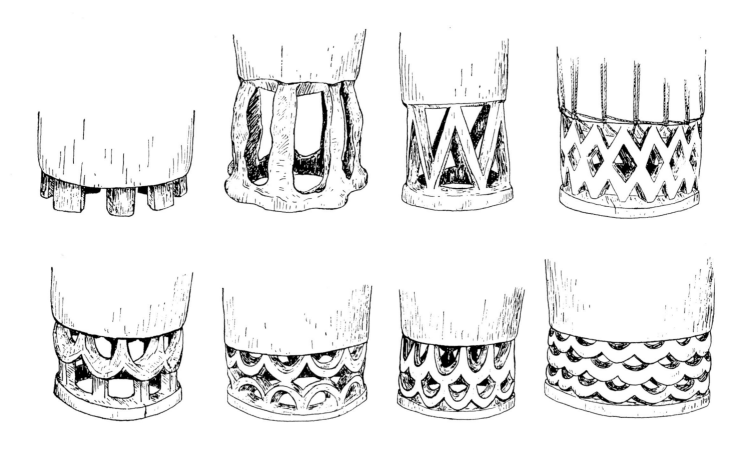

Pahu designs. *Bishop Museum.*

is probably one of the most common designs on a *pahu*. It symbolizes the ancestors' spirits that are always in shadow on the *pahu*, watching out for you.

I put a sharkskin head on my first *pahu*. My father and my uncles helped me. I was really excited and thrilled when we got the sharkskin. I remember how difficult it was to scrape all the meat off it. It's hard to get a sharkskin. Fisher-

men don't like to catch shark because, if they do, the smell stays in the net and later other fish won't come into their net.

Next I had to find a name. It's important that the *pahu* is named, but I didn't know where to find one, or if the name would meet the approval of my teachers and my grandmother, or if I would be satisfied with the name later. I remember really agonizing over that. I can't remember how long it took me, but I know it was several months. The name that I chose for my first *pahu* was Kamakahelei (kah-mah-kah-heh-lay),

❀ VOICE OF THE GODS ❀

Native Hawaiians have long honored the spirit in all things, and have paid homage to their *aliʻi* (ah-LEE-EE) (chiefs) as descendants of the gods. There were, and still are, many gods, great and small. A supreme being presides over all other gods, such as Kane, the creator of all people, Lono, the god of rain and agriculture, and Ku, the god of warriors. Originally, each of the great gods had temples in which they were given appropriate offerings. For example, Lono received pigs and taro; Ku received human sacrifices. The gods are believed to have the powers and passions of humanity, yet to stand above and somewhat apart from people. They might appear in various forms, such as a mist, a plant, a bird, a rock, or a vapor.

"The old Hawaiians believed that the *pahu* was how you spoke to the gods. When you hit the *pahu*—'Boom!'—you were talking back and forth. One of the ways the gods spoke was as thunder. So when you heard the beating of the drum in the temple—'Boom!'—welcoming the day or announcing an event, it was like calling the gods."
—LARRY KAMAHELE

14　HAWAIIAN *PAHU*

which is a family name. It's the name of my great-great-grandmother. She was groomed in the oral traditions and had trained my grandmother, who had trained me. I chose that name for my first *pahu*, hoping that her teachings and her legacy would always be with me and my *pahu*. To me, at that time, it was the obvious foundation, and the *pahu* is your foundation.

My second *pahu*, which I made in my twenties, I haven't named. It's not something I made with a lot of hula emotion. When I made it, I was in an emotional turmoil with myself and my Hawaiian awareness. I never felt that this one ever sounded quite right, so I don't have an attachment to it.

The third *pahu* I made is my largest one. I wanted something bigger. Maybe my ego swelled at that time. I had gone to Oahu. My family is great. I have an uncle who said, "You know, I have a coconut tree if you want to make one of those drums." And I said, "Oh, I'd love to make one." He cut it and the size was just perfect for what I wanted. It's big, but it's light because it dried very well. I struggled getting it past customs going back to Seattle. We wrapped some *lauhala* (lau-HAH-lah), or pandanus mat, around it, and wrapped cardboard around that, and taped it up. I carried it onto the plane, knowing full well it wouldn't fit in those compartments. And then, of course, the flight attendant stopped me and said, "You can't take this!" I said, "Oh, yes, I can. It's a sacred instrument for the hula and it needs to go with me." I think he could tell that I wasn't going to let go

Opposite:
Heiau setting. *Print by Kauanoe.*

Pahu with human figures. *Bishop Museum.*

of it. They took it from me in the plane and put it in a closet where the flight attendants put their belongings. First they wanted to check it in as baggage and I said, "No, it can't go in there."

Back in Seattle, I carved it using modern tools. The geometric designs are obviously made with an electric saw. The center of the design is diamond-shaped, like the four corners of the body, or the four corners of the earth. It's a stylized design of inverted human figures that hold up their arms to symbolize support and foundations. That's my interpretation. The one on the bottom is inverted. You can see human figures with hands and feet on some of the museum pieces that are photographed in books. I stained this *pahu* because, traditionally, people took *kukui* (koo-KOO-ee) soot and oil and rubbed it down so the *pahu* got very black. I used nylon cord instead of sennit, the cord made from the fibers of a coconut husk.

My most recent *pahu*, the one that I use now, I've named Manokalanipo (mah-noh-kah-LAH-nee-poh). Manokalanipo was one of the most influential chiefs of ancient Kaua'i, and did a lot of good things for the people. He's revered in a lot of oral traditions about Kaua'i, so I'm honored to be able to use his name on my *pahu*. People have different ideas about where they're going to draw their names from and about what

responsibilities are going to be imposed with these names. Some believe you shouldn't use names of your ancestors or gods. But the inspiration comes from those legacies and those people who have passed before us, so I have no problem using them.

Treating the *pahu* respectfully

I treat the *pahu* as an ancestor. When they're transported, no matter where, they're completely covered. My mother, bless her heart, has made quilted bags that fit them. She put hula designs on the outside of the bags. The *pahu* are quite well dressed when they go out. I don't allow anything to be put on top of them because they are, like I said, the voice of the gods. When you transport them, you pick them up from the side and the bottom, because you're carrying an ancestor. If you carry it sideways by the hole, to me, that's disrespectful. When you place them onstage, or outside, you need something to put them on, even if it's a thin pad, like a place mat—something to show respect. Just like when you put a baby down, you put it on a baby blanket.

Protocol says you need to earn your right to make the *pahu* sound, to make it talk, to use it. A lot of times when you go to performances, people cannot resist coming up and going "dum-dum-dum." Sometimes that grates on my nerves, but, on the other hand, I need to be understanding that other people don't know. If I hear them or see them, and if I'm there, they stop and go away. I was at a folk festival, and there was a

'Iwalani Christian with her *pahu* in its traveling bag.
Photograph © 1998 Sam Van Fleet.

drummer who had never seen a Hawaiian drum before. He said, "I want to see how one plays this." Our beats are so simplified compared to beats of other cultures, but he wanted to do his African beat on my drum, and I said, "Well, our drums, our beats, are very simple." And he said, "Oh, let me try!" and I thought, "Ugh." I thought, "Boy, you're expanding your horizons here, letting him go on." I'm sure the early Hawaiian voyagers went places where they had to indulge other cultures as well. But the hard thing is when you're in public. Unfortunately, not all of our presentations are culturally focused. At some of our parties, people come and place things, like their drinks, on our drums. If I say,

"Oh, please don't do that, this is a sacred instrument to us," most of them respect that.

An emotion that I get from the *pahu*, and it happens often, is that I feel they talk to me. I know that the skin stretches with the change in temperature in the room and sometimes, all on their own, they'll pop. They'll go "Boom!" I'll be sitting, and all of a sudden—"Boom!" "Boom!" I have them in the hallway so the sun can't get them. But every once in a while they'll go "Boom!" and I'll say, "Mano is talking to me." Sometimes it's that reminder that it's been a while since I've played my *pahu*. It's as if they are saying, "I want to talk. I want to *kani* [KAH-nee]. I want to sound." So I'm sensitive to that.

2 HAWAIIAN *PAHU*

Foundation of the Hula

MOODETTE KAʻAPANA

"The pahu *is the symbol of the* kumu, *or hula master. It's the symbol of the beginning of the hula tradition for the Hawaiian people because it was brought over from Kahiki, or Tahiti, to the Hawaiian Islands. It was the first sound of drumming and the first type of sound that was used for hula. It's the foundation. It's the one. If no other instruments had evolved in our culture, that one instrument, the* pahu, *would always be there. Our whole culture, our whole dance art form, is able to continue because of the* pahu *and nothing else. By itself, it can hold up the rest of our art forms, and even Hawaiian religious rituals."*
—MOODETTE KAʻAPANA

A lifelong dream

Hula is my biggest accomplishment. It was a lifelong dream I had since I was in high school, although I started dancing when I was a child in

Opposite:
Pahu. *Photograph © 1999 Sam Van Fleet.*

Moodette Kaʻapana. *Photograph © 2000 Mary Randlett.*

Honolulu. I didn't have anybody in my family who was a teacher. And so, when I started studying as a child with Auntie Maiki, I pretty much fell in love with her. She made me really appreciate my culture and who I was. We had become so Westernized. After meeting her in 1962, I thought, "It's okay, it's pretty cool to be Hawaiian." She made us really appreciate who we were, but also made us study and realize that there are traditions out there that we can't explain but are part of us, and we should know them.

I knew that I was going away to college, so I figured, "Okay, I'm going to be in college for four years. Then I'll come back and go back to hula, and life will go on that way." But it didn't. I first came to Seattle in 1972 to go to Seattle University. I was going to go home right after graduation. The first year in college was very

rough. I didn't think I was going to make it. But I told my dad that I would do at least one year. I was the oldest, and it was important for me to at least try so that everybody else would have the opportunity to go. And then I ended up staying the summer after my first year because I started dancing with a hula troupe. On the weekends we did shows. It was pretty cool. And then I finished school and got a job. And here I am.

But luckily, while I was at Seattle University, Auntie Maiki always allowed me to go back to the *halau* (hah-LAU), the hula school, every time I went home for vacations. Auntie Mae was her right-hand person, and Auntie Mae's daughter was at Seattle University with me. We danced together here in Seattle. I had to train in Hawai'i because that's where my hula school was. There was no one in Seattle who could finish me in the same hula line. Auntie Maiki passed away, and the only other person I could ask to help me finish was Auntie Mae, so I asked her. I had talked to her several times over the years about

Eleanor Hiram plays the *pahu* while her dancers perform "Kaulilua," 1947. *Bishop Museum.*

coming back and training as a *kumu* (KOO-moo). Even when I was in Seattle, she knew what I was doing all the time. It wasn't like being away from hula school for a long time and then just coming back and saying, "Hey, I want my degree." Every time I went home I would go back to see her and study with her. I was always "in school," just kind of off-campus. I was flying back and forth from Seattle to Hawai'i, staying in Hawai'i for two to three months at a time.

So, things just kind of happened. They flowed for me. I came a long distance to complete my studies, making major sacrifices. I was thirty-nine, not young, but I decided to go back to Hawai'i and settle down and do it. My *kumu* felt that it was time to go ahead and bring me in and finish me off as a *kumu*. So that's how it started.

Making the first *pahu*

I didn't have a *pahu* (PAH-hoo) until I finished my studies as a *kumu*. You have to make your first *pahu* before you can graduate. It's very important that you never use or have a *pahu* until you're in training to be a *kumu*. I have only one *pahu* and it's the one I made myself while I was training, so it's very, very important to me. Now, if I want to, I can go and ask someone else to make one for me. I can buy one from a hula instrument supplier. I can have four, five, six, if I want. But that first one will always be the most important. It's a symbol that my *halau* is now established. So, it's an important symbol and instrument for my students as well.

I made my *pahu* in Kaneohe, Honolulu, at the home of my *kumu hula*, Mae Kamamalu Klein, and her husband Henry Klein. It's made out of

ulu (OO-loo), a breadfruit tree. I could choose any kind of wood I wanted. It was up to me to research and see what was used. Traditionally, they used coconut or *ulu*, and sometimes harder woods. I originally wanted to make a mango drum, but it's a hard wood and I was reminded by my teacher that I wouldn't be allowed to use electric tools. She didn't say no to the mango, but just reminded me, "Think about this now." My parents wanted to cut down a mango tree at our old house, but it wasn't seasoned enough. And I couldn't find a coconut trunk. Wally Akeo, a friend of our family, said, "We just had a storm and all the *ulu* trees fell down." He went up to the house to help clear the yard and brought down an *ulu* piece for me. That's how I got it.

I did everything manually, using a chisel, hammer, mallet, sandpaper, rasps, files, and everything. The only time I could use electricity was when I was getting ready to cut my design out and was allowed to use a drill just to make notches so that the jigsaw could go in and cut it out. When that was done I finished everything by sanding it down. And then I had to find the skin, the *ili* (EE-lee). I was looking for tiger-shark skin because that was the traditional skin used. But with one person who was trying to find a skin for me, we could never connect, and with the other person, who had found one, a cat got to it while it was drying. So I thought, "It's not clicking here." And I had to finish. I only had a couple more weeks before I was going into ceremony. An uncle said, "Well, go ahead and use *pipi* [PEE-pee]," or calfskin. So I said, "Okay, I'm going to use calf." He had a piece that was perfect and gave it to me.

Section of breadfruit tree for Moodette's *pahu*. *Photograph courtesy of Moodette Ka'apana.*

The design drawn onto the wood. *Photograph courtesy of Moodette Ka'apana.*

We found out that it was better to have calfskin, because I was going to be in Washington and the drum was going to be in weather that changed from hot to cold, but was mainly cold, and would be in a house warmed by a heater. When the hula dancers traveled from Hawai'i to the mainland to do shows, especially in the winter time, they had some instances where the skin either warped or cracked. It just expanded and wouldn't soften up. The calfskin is much thicker, so as long as I can keep it damp before I use it, it's doing just fine. Not finding the sharkskin was like a blessing in disguise. It took me about a

Left:
Cutting out the design with an electric jigsaw. *Photograph courtesy of Moodette Ka'apana.*

Below left:
Cutting the calfskin. *Photograph courtesy of Moodette Ka'apana.*

Above:
Attaching the calfskin to the drum. *Photograph courtesy of Moodette Ka'apana.*

month, altogether, to make the drum. I finished it in October of '93. Right after I finished my drum, I came back to Washington, performed at the Folklife Festival, and went back to Hawai'i to get ready for my graduation ceremonies. I finished my hula training in June of '94.

I remember that I finished my drum in '93, because there was still one more year before I got to the part of my training where I could play it. But, since I finished it, I had to bring it back to Seattle with me. I said, "I'm going to leave it in my hula bag." Auntie Mae said, "No, you take it out and look at it." I looked at it for a year. For a whole year I had it downstairs, and didn't play it. I could touch it and rub it, but not hit it. I caressed it, gave it some life. Like you take care of plants, or talk to a baby. But I couldn't hit it or play it, or anything like that. And then, finally, Auntie Mae said, "Bring your *pahu* this time." "Okay," I sighed, because I was finally going to get to use it.

Creating the design

When you're making your drum, you can use any design you want, either traditional, like on the *pahu* that are in museums or on the ones the drum makers make, or nontraditional. You just have to be able to explain it and be very careful about what you use. You can't make it too intricate because simplicity is really important. And it should be something that means something to you. It doesn't have to mean anything to anyone else.

The design on my *pahu* is not traditional. It's a design that I created to signify what the whole experience meant to me, the experience

Petroglyph at Kamooalii. *Bishop Museum.*

of training for *kumu* and earning the right to have this *pahu*. My *pahu* has a design that alternates between a male petroglyph figure and a mountain with two rays coming into the mountain like a "V." And so it goes petroglyph-mountain-petroglyph-mountain. The petroglyphs represent the people who supported me. Their hands are held up, not only to support me, but also to give thanks. And the mountains are the obstacles. But the two rays at the top of the mountain are the inspiration that made me focus on the top, on the summit, because that's where I wanted to be. I was climbing the mountain to reach the summit, always remaining focused.

I spent a lot of time thinking about my design. I drew a lot of different things and I had

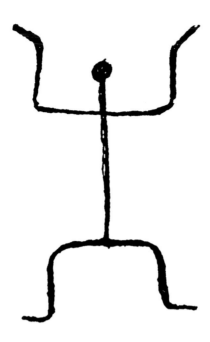

Petroglyph figure *puako:* "I took the concept of balance, but made it stronger by making it a fuller body."

Moodette's *pahu.* *Photograph © 1999 Sam Van Fleet.*

to picture them on the log. I had to keep drawing on paper and wrapping the paper around the log. Everything had to come around and fit correctly. I measured the circumference. If the mountain was this long, then the petroglyph's arms had to be a certain length, and I had to make them connect. I looked at many samples and thought, "No, I don't think this works." I fine-tuned my design for a long time.

You have to decide how many crescents you want to go around the drum, or how many diamonds or squares. You have to be able to say why you're picking that number. People want specific amounts, like twenty-two squares, because they mean something. When I picked the human figures, I picked six. The number was important because it represented God, family, *halau, kumu,* my own *halau,* and my students.

You also have to keep in mind, especially if you're using a nontraditional design, how your lashing is going to go, because the design holds the lashing. If your design doesn't have the right points for the lashing, when you go to lash it either your design will be blocked or there's not going to be any place to hold the lashing. So you have to keep that in mind, too.

It's a lot harder than people think. That's why some people go for the traditional designs. You can look in a book and say, "I want the one with the crescents." And, if nothing else, you can go to the Bishop Museum and count the number of rows, and scale it down to what you need. You know exactly how they lashed it. You can use any drum design that has been pictured or exhibited. But when you're making your own design, it's a lot more involved. That's why I say, "I know my drum intimately." There was a lot of work and thought that went into it.

Choosing a name

I chose the name Nanaikalani (nah-nye-kah-LAH-nee)—"Look to the Heavens"—for my *pahu* because the *pahu* always made me look up to God for focus, strength, and inspiration to continue my work. Every time I look at it, I look up to God and give thanks. Not only do I give thanks now, but at that time I always thought, "Please help me do this." I also feel thankful for having had the opportunity to do that. I didn't want to name it "Look to God," because I didn't want to put a deity in it. But I felt that everyone would appreciate what "Look to the Heavens" means—anybody who has worked towards something. We're always saying "God help me." I have relatives and an older brother who passed away, so I have family spirits that I believe are up there helping me. So I wasn't just looking to God but to everybody up there to help me through this. And they did.

It took me a while to come up with the name, but I just kept rolling the drum around. And one day I saw the petroglyph and the mountain together. Before that I had been looking at them as separate things. I suddenly thought, "That's what it is." Always look up. Look up to God or to the heavens for strength. Never look down. Don't be defeated. Anything is possible as long

as you know where to get your strength from. That's where my *pahu* got its name.

Carrying the *pahu*

Bringing that drum back to Seattle, that's another thing. My teacher said, "You can make your drum as big as you want, but remember you have to carry it. You have to be able to put your arm around it." We were told this all the time. You have to carry it because that's your drum. Without it you're not a teacher. Big and glorious is wonderful for anything else, but your first drum, the one that you're making to become a *kumu*, is the one that's going to be your baby. If you lose anything else, don't lose that drum.

Luckily, the *ulu* trunk that I got was not very big. I think mine was only about twenty-four inches in circumference, and by the time we shaved off the bark on the outside it came down another inch or two to what I have now. And it's only twenty-four inches high. It cannot be higher than your face when you sit down to play it. If it's too tall, you would have to be on your knees. You should be able to sit flat on the ground. Your *pahu* has to be lower than your face so you can see your dancers and so your voice can project out.

Luckily, it fit in the overhead! It was the perfect size. And we made up a little bag for it. We got some fake fur to line the inside, Hawaiian material for the outside, and a drawstring. I just throw it on my back. So it worked out really well that it ended up being the right size for the plane, able to travel. Some other teachers have bigger ones for which they actually have to make crates. When they travel interisland or out of state, they can't carry their *pahu* on the plane. But I can carry mine in the sack right on my back.

Keeping the culture close

Becoming a *kumu* was a very big accomplishment. Some people think, "Okay, now you're a *kumu* and that's it." But that's just the beginning. I recently graduated five of my students as *'olapa* (OH-lah-pah) and *ho'opa'a* (HOH-oh-PAH-ah), the first two levels. So now we are the first *halau* in our hula genealogy to be outside of Hawai'i and to have had an *uniki* (oo-NEE-kee), or graduation ceremony, out of state. And that's the whole purpose, to be able to keep hula, and Auntie Maiki's line of hula, alive in the mainland United States. I had seen so many different lines of dancing come up to the mainland, and once the dancing got up here it was as if they threw everything out the window and created their own thing. I wanted to be able to keep Auntie Maiki's line alive, at least in Washington. It kept my culture close to me. And I was able to share my culture with the people in Washington through hula. The whole point is to continue the tradition and make it an art form. If you don't have a way to perpetuate that art form, then it disappears. It gets diluted. It's gone.

☼ A CULTURAL RENAISSANCE ☼

Today, after more than a century of immigration to Hawai'i from the U.S. mainland, China, Japan, the Philippines, and other Asian nations, Native Hawaiians are a minority in their homeland. Since the 1960s, however, Native Hawaiians have experienced a cultural renaissance, celebrating and renewing their cultural roots and fighting for their identity. Hula is a fundamental part of the renaissance and is highly esteemed. There are now two types of hula: *kahiko* (kah-HEE-koh), or ancient style, and *'auana* (AH-wah-nah), or modern style. In Hawai'i, hotels are now realizing the value of providing *kahiko* performances in addition to *'auana*. Outside of the islands, and especially on the West Coast of the mainland United States, there are dozens of hula schools, each adhering to its own style. The renaissance has even spread as far as Japan, Mexico, and Europe. Hawaiian *kumu hula* now fly around the world to teach hula to Japanese, Mexicans, and Europeans. In 1997, a Japanese group won first place at the annual World Hula Competition.

Above:

Students at Moodette's (seated, left) graduation ceremony.
Photograph courtesy of Moodette Ka'apana.

Below:

Moodette's genealogy chart. *Courtesy of Moodette Ka'apana.*

Keahi Luahine
|
Mary Kawena Pukui
|
Lokalia Montgomery
|
Kekauilani Kalama   Ma'iki Aiu Lake   Sally Woods Nalua'i
                           |
                    Papa 'Ūniki Lehua
                      (ma Puna) 8-27-73

Mae Kamāmalu Klein   Leina'ala Kalama Heine

Papa 'Ūniki Maile Li'ili'i	**Papa 'Ūniki Kukui**	**Papa 'Ūniki Maile Kaluhea**	**Papa 'Ūniki Maile Kaluhea**	**Papa 'Ūniki Liko Lehua**
8-18-85	12-30-90	8-11-91	5-3-92	6-25-94
Nā Kumu Hula	*Kumu Hula*	*Nā Kumu Hula*	*Kumu Hula*	*Nā Kumu Hula*
Michael Pili Pang	Racine Maka Klein	Patrick Uaaokapuwehi Choy	Abigail Lehua Galuteria	Billie Kamaha'o Klein-Oda
April Pualani Chock		Ardis Ku'ulei Gomes		Moodette Keli'iho'omalu-Ka'apana
		Danielle Pohai Stone		
Nā Novice 'Olapa	*Nā Novice 'Olapa*	Ab Kawainoho Valencia		*Nā 'Olapa*
Michelle Nalei Akina	Alva Kaipo Kamalani			Carol Namahana Kwan-Young
Naomi Kahakuhaupio Lake	Bernette Ipolani Moss	*Nā Ho'opa'a*		Beverly Kula Miller
Tsu Lan Kaleilehua Lopez	Cherise Keala Mundon	Abigail Lehua Galuteria		Susan Pua O'Mahoney
		Kumiko Kanani Honda		Alena Kealohilani Stone
		Mariko Ha'aha'a Honda		Ramona La'iku Stutzmann
				Ronette Leiola Souza
		Nā 'Olapa		Ella Kawahine Tokunaga
		Sommer Kanoe Galuteria		
		Amber Kanani Gomes		
		Tanya mahea Kobashigawa		

Papa 'Ūniki Liko Lehua
6-25-94

Nā 'Olapa
Jaqueline Kehau Brackbill
Elizabeth Keikilani Curnan
Alva Kaipoleimanu Kamalani
Bernette Ipolani Moss
Cherise Keala Mundon
Wendi Pa'ahana Roehrig
Pat Kalaniumi Roxburgh
June Kaililani Tanoue

3 SAMOAN *TĀNOA*

A Visible Symbol of Community

VERONICA LEASIOLAGI BARBER and SAPINA PELE

"Since the tānoa *is round and its legs represent the ancestors or noble families of Samoa, it can be seen as a visible symbol of community for Samoans, both those living in the islands and those of us who live in the United States."*
—VERONICA LEASIOLAGI BARBER

"The tānoa *is an object that every Samoan immediately knows is Samoan. For me, it's a symbol of who I am. It's about where I come from and who we are as a people. A few years ago I was in Samoa for the South Pacific Mini Games. At the closing ceremonies, the Samoan museum gave gifts to all the dignitaries who had come from the various islands. Everybody got some* siapo, *or bark cloth, and a* tānoa. *It was nice to see them use the* tānoa *as a symbol of who we are."*—SAPINA PELE

Opposite:
Tānoa. *Burke Museum collection. Photograph © 1999 Sam Van Fleet.*

Veronica Leasiolagi Barber. *Photograph by Jerry Lynne Barber.*

Sapina Pele. *Photograph © 2000 Mary Randlett.*

Used for many occasions

The *tānoa* (TAH-noh-ah), or *'ava* (AH-vah) bowl, is a round wooden bowl that is at the center of the Samoan *'ava* [kava] ceremony. This ceremony is at the heart of Samoan community life, which includes the welcoming of others into your home and community. The *tānoa* is only one element of the ceremony, which also includes *'ava* roots, the *'ava* cup, the *'ava* strainer, the gathering of village chiefs, speeches, the *taupou* or village maiden who mixes the *'ava*, the *tautu* or tattooed young man who serves the *'ava*, and the orators for the *'ava*.

'Ava plant and root (*Piper methysticum*). *Illustration by Joan Fleming, from Lois Lucas,* Plants of Old Hawaii *(Honolulu: The Bess Press, 1982).*

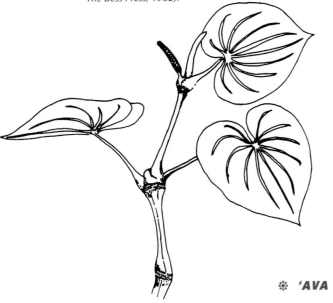

The *tānoa*, used for mixing and serving *'ava*, is a powerful symbol in Samoan tradition. It speaks to relationships, to welcoming, to human dignity, to the need for community, to neighborly love, and to harmonious living. It's often used on a daily basis by the *matais* (mah-TYES) (chiefs) when they sit around and drink *'ava*, discussing the affairs of the extended families or villages. But it's especially used at formal ceremonies, like welcoming visitors, starting important meetings and celebrations, dedicating new building facilities, or bestowing chiefly titles to indicate the transition of power. The *tānoa* also has religious significance. It's related to and sometimes used in the Christian Catholic tradition of drinking from the one cup of Christ at Mass or Eucharistic celebration. For a long time Samoans, too, drank from one *'ava* cup around the *tānoa*.

The *tānoa* is used to mix the *'ava* for reconciliation when people have conflicts in their relationship. For example, in Samoa, if one person offends another, the offender's senior *matai* gathers his family and goes to apologize to the other person's family. The *matai* leads a delegation of young men armed with weapons, ready to have a fight if not forgiven. He sits in front of the other person's house with a fine mat covering his head. Meanwhile, the chiefs and people of the other side have gathered in the house and

☼ 'AVA ☼

Known in English as kava, *'ava*, is made from *Piper methysticum*, a woody shrub that grows up to four meters high. Native to Melanesia, *'ava* was introduced by early voyagers to Polynesia, where it now thrives in wet, shady places. Since only male plants are known (except in Vanuatu, where female plants exist as well), kava is unable to reproduce itself and must be propagated by humans.

At the head of a Samoan family organization is a senior *matai*, a high chief who holds a traditional title through which the family traces its history. But each extended family has more than one *matai*. The senior *matai* is supported by several junior high chiefs along with talking chiefs (a special class of chiefs responsible for oratory at gatherings and func- tions). The selection of the *matai* title holders is up to the extended family. Some junior titles can be appointed by the senior *matai*, but the senior *matai* must have the agreement of all branches of the extended family. All *matai* honor their titles by serving their families. They have many responsibilities, including gathering the resources necessary for weddings, funer- als, investitures of new titles, and dedications of new meetinghouses or churches, as well as overseeing the use of communal land, settling disputes, and motivating work and service for the common good.

Left:
Talking chief, Faleu, Manono, Western Samoa, 1996.
Photograph by James Cooper Abbott.

Above:
Men sitting around a *tānoa* (with bucket for water), Samoa.
Photograph by Veronica Leasiolagi Barber.

are debating whether to forgive the offending side or not. If the decision is made to accept the reconciliation, the chief in the house comes out and presents a stylized speech, removes the fine mat, folds it, and helps the seated *matai* to stand up. They hug and shake hands, and the offender's *matai* is invited into the house. To complete the reconciliation there is an *'ava* ceremony. A *tānoa* is placed in the center back half of the house, attended to by the *taupou*

❀ PREPARING AND DRINKING 'AVA ❀

For centuries, *Piper methysticum* roots have been used to prepare a mildly narcotic beverage. The entire plant is dug up and the roots are split into pieces. Large pieces of root, with part of the stem attached, are the *tugase* (too-GAH-seh) that Samoans give to visitors of high rank. Tender young roots make the best *'ava* and are used as they are. Large older roots first must be grated, crushed, or chewed before they can be mixed with water to produce a watery, light brown drink that has a slightly bitter, peppery taste, numbing to the mouth and tongue. In sufficient quantities, it is mildly paralyzing and creates a euphoric but clear-minded state. In Samoa *'ava* is traditionally drunk mostly in ceremonies. Today it is also drunk more commonly, as one can see in the open markets.

(TAU-poh), who begins to mix the *'ava* in it. Speeches of forgiveness and renewed friendship are exchanged by the chiefs of both sides. The *'ava* is mixed with water in the *tānoa*, and, when it is ready, the orator announces this fact while clapping. The *'ava* is then served by dipping the cup into the *tānoa* and presenting it to the *matais* on both sides, as prescribed by the orator. Those receiving the *'ava* pour a drop back to mother earth to acknowledge where it came from, and lift the *'ava* cup slightly upward to the level of the forehead, saying words like, "May this *'ava*

'Ava roots gathered for a ceremony, Aasu, Tutuila, American Samoa, 1992. *Photograph by Anthony Fitiafiafi Barber.*

Man making _tānoa_, Samoa, 1950s. _Photograph reproduced courtesy of Matson Navigation Company._

bring reconciliation to the situation at hand" or "May this _'ava_ continue to remind us of the importance of forgiving mistakes and beginning life anew." "_Ia manuia!_" (EE-yah mah-NOO-ee-yah) (Blessings!) The people reply, "_Ia soifua!_" (EE-yah soy-FOO-ee-yah) (Long life!)

Not an ordinary object

Making a _tānoa_ is not like making a canoe or house, where only special people can make it. It's open to anybody who has the time, the skill, and the piece of hard wood to carve one. Whatever hard wood is available on the islands is what people use.

Not every Samoan household has a _tānoa_ that can be used for an _'ava_ ceremony. The ceremony requires a medium- or large-size _tānoa_ and they're not easy to get. You can find them at certain markets back home, but they're expensive. A big _tānoa_ usually has been given to its owner as a gift from the extended family. It's the

responsibility of the talking chief to have at least one _tānoa_ for use by his _matai_ when the occasion calls for it. If you don't have a _tānoa_ when you need one, you can usually borrow one from your neighbors, if you live in Samoa. They will be more than willing to lend you one. This practice is more difficult to realize in the United States, where families live far apart. In this case, a _matai_ makes sure he or she has a _tānoa_ on hand before the need arises.

"My father has two _tānoa_, a big one and a medium one. They were given to him by special _matais_ back home. I'd like a big one, but my small one is precious to me because it was given to me when I went to Samoa in the early '70s. If I had a big _tānoa_ and someone said, 'Sapina, we have to have an _'ava_ ceremony,' I'd let them use it. But because I'm just an ordinary citizen, I wouldn't think of using mine for a special ceremony unless I were asked to. But if you only have a little one like I have, no one is going to ask to borrow it anyway!"—SAPINA PELE

"I have a big _tānoa_. I got it when I got married. I asked my oldest brother to bring me one as a wedding gift. Since I'm a _matai_, I wanted to be sure I had one. I took my _tānoa_ all over the world when my husband and I were traveling with the U.S. Army. I used it to mix and serve punch for officers' wives when they came to my house for refreshments. I've also used it to decorate the entryway in my home, which inevitably makes it a conversation piece. I've used it to mix _'ava_ for the Council of Chiefs in Hawai'i, for bestowing new chief titles, and for welcoming special visitors. And, yes, I've also loaned my _tānoa_ to others when they ask to borrow it."
—VERONICA LEASIOLAGI BARBER

"In my home in Seattle, I don't use my small *tānoa* for anything other than decoration. It's something that I put out and people ask me about it. It gives me an opportunity to talk about Samoa. Sometimes I have it sitting in my office at school. I have toys in it that I use with the kids. It's a piece to open the kids up. If I want the kids to talk, I'll ask them, 'How many legs does it have?' or 'What does it look like to you?' It depends on the individual and how they want to use it and display it. But, definitely, if non-Samoans come into a Samoan's house and see a *tānoa*, they ask, 'What's that?'"—SAPINA PELE

Traditionally, a *tānoa* was supposed to be hung up when you weren't using it. That's why there's a rope attached to it. The traditional Samoan house has only a small amount of shelf space right beneath the roof. Rolled-up mats are usually stored in this space during the day and laid out at night for sleeping. Things with handles, like the *tānoa* or baskets, are hung to keep them off the ground and to keep animals from getting into them. Leaving a *tānoa* sitting on the ground is an invitation for a cat to climb in and use it as a nice, smooth, warm bed.

Samoan house (*fale*), Ta'u Village, American Samoa, 1954. *Photograph by Lowell D. Holmes.*

A symbol of community life

There is a mythology about the *tānoa*. One legend says that each of the legs represents a Samoan ancestor as he gathered with others in a circle around a pit. Another legend says that the *tānoa* was given to Samoans by four noble brothers who separated and founded four different island groups in Polynesia. In some parts of Samoa the *tānoa* has four legs.

"To me, the *tānoa* is symbolic of the circular and connected nature of who we are as Samoans. We conduct daily business and activities facing one another. It is important for us to face one another when we talk because this gives us the opportunity to read nonverbal, as well as verbal, communication. It is also very respectful of the other's humanity. The *'ava* ceremony is full of symbols that affirm and enhance the importance of people, humanity, and relationships. Samoans live their lives in such a way that the importance of the individual is secondary to that of the community. The *tānoa* and the idea of seeing people's legs as they face each other are very communal. At the heart of that community is the extended family. In America today, we're seeing the importance of developing a circular community, whether it be sitting around a dining-room table or meeting and talking in small groups. These efforts attempt to get people to face one another and talk in ways that demonstrate trust and build community. Samoans have always sat in circles, on the floor, of course. But they have always faced and looked at each other when they talk. In some cultures people don't do that."
—VERONICA LEASIOLAGI BARBER

Matai (chiefs) sitting at house posts during village council meeting, Manu'a, American Samoa, 1954. *Photograph by Lowell D. Holmes.*

The fact that the *tānoa* is round also reminds us of the extended family, caring for one another, and looking out for one another. Samoans don't have drop-in centers. Instead, if a youth doesn't like what's going on in his or her home, it would be easy to say, "things aren't going well," and just go to another house and be taken care of. There's a lot of symbolism in the *tānoa* about Samoan family life.

To many Samoans, the legs symbolize the Samoan house, or *fale* (FAH-lay). Samoan houses have two shapes: oval and round. Either shape is built with posts all around the rim to support the roof. When chiefs meet, they sit at the posts inside the house. Only the titled chiefs sit at the posts. The nontitled aren't allowed in the circle, but are consulted by their particular *matai* either before or after the meeting. A *tānoa* is like the house with posts where the *matais* sit and distinguish themselves. They are in a circle and able to talk, yet differentiated according to their ranks.

Samoan Youth Group performing 'ava dance, St. George Catholic Church, Seattle, 1998 (from left to right: Patrick Faleniko, Filipo Ah Ching, Lena Leonato, Melvin Foifua). *Photograph by Veronica Leasiolagi Barber.*

Learning the whole context

The point about the *tānoa*, or any other object you select out of Samoan life, is that it's hard to treat it as an individual piece, separate from everything that goes with it—the 'ava cup, the 'ava strainer, the *taupou* who prepares the 'ava, the *matai* who orates the 'ava, the *tautu* (TAU-too) who serves the 'ava, and the chiefs who gather for the 'ava. The *tānoa* has meaning only in its whole context. But if you pull out an item and try to speak about it without the other objects, then it doesn't have as much meaning, or its meaning gets fragmented and confusing. It's harder to get to the depth of what the *tānoa* means in relation to the other objects, and why it's part of a ritual in Samoan culture. It's important to recognize that.

"When we see a *tānoa* in Seattle, it becomes a lopsided symbol. For example, our kids say, 'Oh, yeah, we have one of those in our house.' If they're asked, 'Well, what is that?' they'll say, 'It's a *tānoa*.' And if you ask, 'What do you do with it?' they'll say, 'Oh, Samoans use it for 'ava.' And that's about the extent of what they'll understand. They don't go deeper. You say, 'Well, let me tell you about it. At one time this bowl represented real people! These were our ancestors who sat around the *tānoa*, and made their 'ava, and then gave the cup to one another. And then over time they created this symbol.' The next generation won't be able to speak about it with conviction and passion. It becomes a passive object in the house. Today, kids are lucky if they can say, 'Well, that's a *tānoa*.' But if you ask, 'How do you spell it?' they'll say, 'I don't know.'"—SAPINA PELE

When I recently did a dance with the youth group, a dance called the 'ava, it was really important to use a *tānoa*. When we did that number, we learned the

❁ TRANSLATING CHIEFLY ROLES IN THE UNITED STATES ❁

Changes arise when Samoans try to maintain the *matai* system and its customs outside of Samoa. A *matai* living in the United States has authority within his extended family, but the role is not as clearly defined as in Samoa. Much of the *matai's* traditional role has to do with settling disputes over land. Family ownership of land, however, does not transfer to America. Knowing one's place in the social scheme has always been important in Samoan culture. The absence of traditional authority and leadership is one of the important cultural differences that Samoans face as they adjust to life in the United States.

words and sang the song. It's about how the *'ava* is used, how it's served, and how the *taupou* is supposed to act in making the *'ava*. A lot of the kids had heard about a *tānoa*, but some of them had never seen one. So it was very important for me that we each had a *tānoa* when we performed it for the first time. We had to go out and borrow them. We even borrowed some from the Burke Museum! The *tānoa* has more meaning for me since we performed that number because it provided a learning opportunity for some of the kids. But although the kids know it's a *tānoa* and that it's used for *'ava*, they don't have the passion for it that I have."—SAPINA PELE

It's important to recognize that Samoan culture is passed on through active involvement and experience, not through classes in schools. Without the opportunity to experience the culture as it is lived in the islands, the Samoans in the United States, especially those who are born here, are not able to fully understand. That includes their understanding of what a *tānoa* is. It's not fair to expect young people to know all about these things, since this knowledge is learned over time and in the proper context of events like weddings, funerals, investiture of *matai* titles, and the receiving of visitors. These are all occasions that set the context for teaching and passing on the culture.

The longer you stay away from your homeland, the more it dilutes your passion for your culture. It's important to teach our next generation. It's not that they don't want to know. But, as adults today, we don't give them the information they need to develop that kind of passion. As adults in this society, we don't have the time. These are different times. We may have to use new technology. A *tānoa* Web site!

4 MAORI *KOROWAI*

Mantle of Status

AOTAUMAREWA LORRAINE ELKINGTON MOREHOUSE

"The korowai, *or cloak, is made from the materials of the land from which we come. These strands are woven together to keep us warm and to show our status. A cloak touches the most important celebrations in a Maori person's life: weddings and funerals. How it is worn depends on the occasion and the status of the person. Usually it's the eldest of the tribe or the family who wears the* korowai. *When you go onto the* marae, *the gathering area in a Maori village, chieftain's families have a representative on the* paepae, *or dignitaries' platform. That's where the eldest male wears his* korowai."

—AOTAUMAREWA LORRAINE ELKINGTON MOREHOUSE

Opposite:

Feather cloak made by Mereana Ngatai. *Burke Museum collection. Photograph © 2000 Sam Van Fleet.*

Aotaumarewa Lorraine Elkington Morehouse. *Photograph © 2000 Mary Randlett.*

Lorraine's grandfather, Ariki Pere Wineera, wearing the family *korowai*, 1980s. *Photograph courtesy of Lorraine Morehouse.*

Lorraine's grandmother, Ramari Paraoni Te Hiko Wineera, wearing the family *korowai*, 1980s. *Photograph courtesy of Lorraine Morehouse.*

My family's cloak

In one photo, my grandfather (my mother's father) is wearing the *korowai* (ᴋᴏʜ-roh-wye) that has been in our family for generations. In the other photo, my grandmother (my mother's mother) is wearing the same *korowai*. She's wearing the cloak because it was the opening of her tribal meetinghouse and she was the eldest woman. Her father gave the land on which the house was built, so she was chosen to be the first woman in the meetinghouse for its dedication. To show her status she wore the cloak.

A cloak is handed down from one generation to another, always to the eldest person, and usually the eldest son. This one was handed down through my mother's father's father, the Wineera line. It was passed down to my grandmother after my grandfather died. In my grandmother's case, she was the eldest woman, so my uncle respected that.

The cloak she is wearing in the photo is now in a museum in New York. Apparently, my mother's family got together and talked about what to do with the cloak. They unanimously decided that if they put it in the museum, it would be cared for, whereas if they just kept it hanging on the wall (my grandmother always hung it on the wall, just stretched out flat), it could deteriorate. So they saw this as a means of preserving it and of letting other people see it. If it hadn't gone into the museum, it would have been passed down to my uncle. I'm not sure he appreciated the *korowai*—he was young at the time—so the family turned it over to the museum. He didn't appreciate the gift—and it

❀ SETTLING NEW ZEALAND ❀

The Maori are Polynesians who sailed from other parts of Polynesia about 1,200 years ago to the islands they called Aotearoa—Land of the Long White Cloud—the last Polynesian islands to be settled. Now known as New Zealand, these islands had a cooler climate than other parts of Polynesia, and presented the new settlers with different natural resources that in turn required different types of garments for keeping warm and shielding from the rain—including various types of cloaks.

"Settling New Zealand. All the leaders are wearing *korowai*. It's important for everyone to see who is giving the orders" (Lorraine Morehouse). *War Canoe of New Zealand* Sydney Parkinson, 1784.
Alexander Turnbull Library, National Library of New Zealand, Te Puna Matauranga o Aotearoa.

❀ ENGLISH DOMINATION ❀

The first European to visit Aotearoa was Captain James Cook, who arrived in 1769. English missionaries arrived in the early 1800s. In 1840, English government officials and Maori chiefs signed the Waitangi (WYE-tahng-ee) Treaty, making New Zealand a British colony. In the following decades, there were many battles between Maori and Europeans for control of land. The strong warrior tradition and sophisticated fortifications of the Maori enabled them to hold out for long periods, but eventually they were subdued. As English culture came to dominate the islands, Maori customs changed and certain things were lost. The Maori language was banned, and a whole generation grew up forbidden to speak it. In the early 1970s, however, efforts were made to revive it, using elders to teach the young children in *kohanga reo*, or language nests (preschools).

Korowai draped over casket at funeral of Tohurua Parata of **Waikanae, New Zealand, 1932.** *Photograph by William Hall Raine. Collection of the Museum of New Zealand Te Papa Tongarewa.*

is a gift. I think he's changed now. He's gotten older, and with that comes more understanding.

Wrapping a person with love

When I was growing up in the '50s in New Zealand, so many of the traditions were being let go. They're being brought back now. I remember that when I was young there was a wedding ceremony, and in that ceremony the families of the bride and groom exchanged *korowai* and put them around one another. If my daughter was marrying a man from your family, I'd put my *korowai* around your son, and you'd put yours around my daughter. That's part of the ceremony. The *korowai* is a symbol that means "may my love keep you warm and envelop all of you." It would be worn at the wedding as a token of acceptance and love and all the emotions that go into accepting a person and wishing them well in their lives. They used *korowai* for funerals, too. If somebody in the family died, family members would place one of their *korowai* over the casket. If the cloak was placed face down, it would get buried with the person. Otherwise, it would be handed down. That was a common thing when I was growing up. If there was a death, I always saw the casket with the *korowai* draped over it.

Different types of cloaks

Here, in the United States, you distinguish between a dress and a ball gown. It's like that

☀ CLOAKS EXIST IN MANY STYLES ☀

There are many types of cloaks, the general name for which is *kakahu* (KAH-kah-hoo). They are categorized according to their form of decoration and the occasions upon which they are worn. Practical rain capes have an outer surface that is thatched with thick layers of plant material, which protect against the wind and shed rainwater. In the past, there were also plain cloaks for warfare. Ceremonial cloaks are more finely woven and elaborate. They may be decorated with a *tāniko* border done in a traditional twining technique. Plain fiber cloaks decorated with a colored *tāniko* border on the sides are known as *kaitaka* (KYE-tah-kah). Cloaks adorned with pom-poms, tassels, long fringes of hand-rolled *muka* (MOO-kah) (fine inner flax fibers), or strips of dog fur are called *korowai*. Cloaks decorated with feathers, or *kahu huruhuru* (KAH-hoo HOO-roo-HOO-roo), are the most prestigious type of cloak and are worn for important ceremonial occasions.

with cloaks. There are different types. There are some that are used daily and some that are used for ceremonies. Those are two different things. There are cloaks that you use every day to keep warm, like a blanket, which are made of wool or flax. It looks nice. It pleases the eye. It's just an article of clothing; it's not ceremonial.

Left:
Kiwi feather cloak. *Photograph © Brian Brake.*

Center:
Rain cape. *Photograph © Brian Brake.*

Right:
***Korowai* with tassels.** *Photograph © Brian Brake.*

❁ WEAVING WITHOUT LOOMS ❁

Maori have never had looms. Instead, they use a finger-weaving technique with warp and weft threads that is similar to European twining. The weaving is usually tied between two sticks and allowed to hang free while the weaver—always a woman—works. Much energy goes into gathering and preparing the materials. To make a ceremonial cloak, for instance, a weaver needs about eight months, at least three of which are spent on preparation. Generally, Maori view weaving as a sacred art; the artist is a vehicle through whom the gods create. Weaving is a state of being into which the weaver is initiated with prayer and ceremony. She must concentrate and clear her mind so that her spirit, mind, and physical being are in tune with one another. To fully understand this state of being, a student needs to work with a master weaver who is prepared to share her knowledge. Styles of weaving are not rigidly fixed but always leave room for individual invention. Patterns and colors are rich in symbolism and hidden meaning.

Digger Te Kanawa weaving a feather cloak, Waitomo, 1993. *Photograph by Richard L. Taylor.*

Cloak with *tāniko* border. *Photograph © Brian Brake.*

Women Weaving, Gottfried Lindauer, ca. 1906, oil on canvas. *Auckland Art Gallery, Toi o Tāmaki.*

The main material used for weaving is native New Zealand flax, *Phormium tenax*. A weaver must gather flax judiciously because careful cutting will ensure the plant's continued growth. For instance, a weaver must not cut too closely to the young shoot in the center of the plant. She must trim off the hard end of the leaves and place these at the base of the plant as compost. Once gathered, the flax undergoes a lengthy process of preparation in which the weaver removes the ribs and discolored edges from the leaves; measures and splits the leaves into strips of even widths and lengths; separates the outer green fibers from the inner white fibers by running both sides of the flax over a blunt surface, such as a mussel shell or wire fence; rolls the strands of fiber into bundles of two-ply cord, which are then washed and soaked; and beats them on a flat stone and rubs them to make the fibers soft and pliable. All this must be done for both the warp and weft threads. Dyeing is accomplished with various barks and swamp sediment to produce black, tan, and yellow. Ashes are used to make the dyes colorfast.

New Zealand flax (*Phormium tenax*). *Courtesy of Calderdale Museums and Arts, Bankfield Museum, Halifax, United Kingdom.*

Ceremonial clothing is sacred. The type of ceremonial cloak my grandparents are wearing in the photos is different from the one that you wear daily. It has tassels. When you see a person wearing a ceremonial cloak with feathers and tassels, it is called a *korowai*. You automatically think of someone with high status. Usually, the *korowai* has *tāniko* (TAH-nee-koh), like needlepoint, around the border, and the pattern and colors are those of your tribe or family. Sometimes you see a lot of white and black and red, or green or blue. If you were someone of great importance, you would have kiwi feathers. These feathers look brown, but if you get them in the light they're different colors, blue and green, a bit like duck feathers. A lot of work goes into these, because of the plaiting and having to weave the feathers into the fabric. The fabric used to be made with reeds or flax, and sometimes still is. The flax is scraped until it's really soft and then it's woven. So there's a lot of work going into it. The one my grandmother had is ancient, and as it gets older the flax changes color, from a white to a cream to a bone color.

Earning your status

If I were teaching children the word for *korowai* in a *kohanga reo* (koh-HUHNG-ah RAY-oh), or language nest (preschool), I would teach them how the cloak is used and what kinds of feelings it arouses. People have to be serious-minded when they use the *korowai* for ceremonies. Everything that children learn about has an emotional, social, and spiritual aspect to it. It's a holistic form of learning, where you learn in complete cycles. It's not just facts and figures.

I'd teach them that usually the elders wear the *korowai*. The elders have status because they've gone through life serving the people. They've gone through building the house, cooking in the kitchen, cleaning the latrines, weaving, administering to the sick, and teaching children. If we're having an occasion where we're having a lot of visitors, everybody goes down to the *marae* (mah-RYE) and works to prepare for our visitors' arrival. That happens often. You go down and work for the tribe, for the family, for others. You mow the lawns, clean up, and prepare food. And so, by the time you come to wear a *korowai* on the *paepae* (pye-pye) (where all the dignitaries sit), you've gone through all those stages and you've earned your seat. You don't take your seat on the *paepae* just because you're an old lady or an old man but because you've gone through the stages of serving the people, whose respect you now have. Once you've earned your seat on the *paepae,* you're not allowed back in the kitchen. It's as though we're saying, "You've already done this; now it's our turn to serve you."

So, if I were to teach children, I would tell them that maybe their grandfather, who is on the *paepae* wearing a *korowai*, once learned to do all these other things, just like learning to do his studies in school. I think there's a humility that goes with it. People don't just acquire that seat. If they acquire a seat on the *paepae* it is because the people revere them. And that's their power, or *mana* (MAH-nah). By the time you get to wear a *korowai*, you've earned it. It doesn't matter what kind of professional work you do. If you support and sustain your family, that's what matters. If you serve your fellow human being, that's what matters. That's what gives you status.

☀ THE *MARAE* ☀

The enclosed outdoor space in front of a ceremonial meetinghouse where gatherings are held and visitors are greeted is called the *marae*. In this place of great power and spirituality, Maori customs and values are given ultimate expression. On a *marae*, one has the right to speak as one feels, knowing that others will show their respect by listening without interrupting. Every emotion can be communicated and shared, not only with the living but with one's ancestors as well. It is here that Maori rise in oratory, weep for the dead, pray to the gods, laugh with friends, shelter their guests, gather in meetings, share in feasts, hold weddings and funerals, and celebrate special occasions in song and dance. The people of the land—the hosts—are the foundation of a *marae*. Through their caring for, and sharing with, one another, they contribute to the tradition of the *marae*. Yet they need visitors to serve in order to make the *marae* complete.

Below:

National Marae, Christchurch, 1993. *Photograph by Richard L. Taylor.*

Right:

Illustration of a *marae*. *Courtesy Departments of Maori Studies and Anthropology, University of Auckland, New Zealand.*

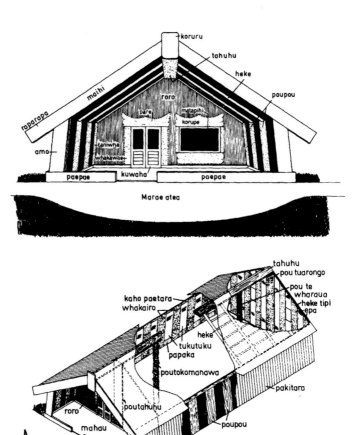

Children learning in a *kohanga reo* (language nest), Tutarawananga, New Zealand. *Photograph courtesy of Mana Magazine.*

It's hard for some people in the white community in New Zealand to understand when they see Maori people doing physical jobs, like working down on the wharf getting their hands dirty, and then see them going onto a *marae* in the village and see people revering them. But it's because they have served the people that they have earned that respect.

As a Maori woman, if I see somebody wearing a *korowai*, I relate differently to the person. There's a lot more respect there. It's not that you diminish anybody who doesn't wear a *korowai*, by any means. It just means that if I saw an old person, I'd give them the respect they deserve. Whatever they needed, their request would be granted. If they asked something of me, I would be more than happy to do it. I'd know

that somewhere along the line they had done it for others. And now is my time to show love for them and appreciation for what they've done. A lot of these old people are like landmarks, like a standard to look up to, a model to emulate. They are the type of person I would like to be. It's not an easy thing to do. It's a very selfless, giving type of life.

I went through those stages before I left home. When we were little children, my mother would take us to visit people who were sick. And while she was caring for them or talking to them, we would be cleaning house, or doing the laundry, or getting food ready for them. And then we would feed and wash them. My mother made sure that we did this.

Recently, in the younger generation, people try to skip a stage. Usually, they'll try to skip serving the people. They'll skip cleaning the meetinghouse, cooking in the kitchen, even fishing. They'll come onto the *marae* trying to be an

In the late 1800s, in addition to woven cloaks, Maori artists produced doilies, teapot covers, altar cloths, bags, bodices, and hats. But the art of making cloaks, and of weaving in general, lapsed over the years. By the 1930s, cloak making almost died out. Large areas of forest had been cleared to make farms for settlers, and bird populations had dwindled. Many Maori migrated to urban areas, villages were depleted, and flax plantations became overgrown. In recent years, cloak making has been part of a strong Maori cultural revival, which includes language and art. Today a new generation of artists has created innovative cloaks that are still anchored in tradition. Most recently, artists have woven cloaks from materials such as film strips or copper wire.

executive. They'll assume the position. But that's not our true culture. That belongs to a different culture. If individuals do that, they lose the respect of a lot of people.

Traditions are reborn

There's a revival now. Throughout New Zealand there's a revival of the Maori language in the *kohanga reo*. It's quite enlightening to my generation because it was my generation that lost the language. For us to see our children now is really refreshing, strengthening. It gives us a good feeling to know that our children are not going to lose their traditions, because with the language come the traditions.

When traditions are being reborn, so is the clothing that goes with them. New *korowai* are being made today. My cousin, who's visiting from home, has a father who is an elder and an artist. An aunt of mine made him a *korowai* when he became an elder. Now ceremonial cloaks are made out of different materials (I think they use rooster feathers now because they're easiest to get), but that's what life is all about. You take what's available now and use that. It's really good that the art of making *korowai* is being revived. It's a symbol to show you what's happening in New Zealand. The feathered cloak in the "Pacific Voices" exhibit was made by Mereana Ngatai, an artist in New Zealand, for the Burke Museum in Seattle. That's part of the revival. This is great. It's very correct. It's beautiful. It's very pretty. I think any of the elders would be more than happy to wear something like this.

5 MICRONESIAN CANOE

Reminder of a Way of Life

ROKURO MESIAB, with DAVID HAWELMAI

"In Micronesia, canoes have been the main means of transportation for a long time. Here, in the United States, you use trucks or cars to go to work or pick up loads. But in Micronesia, we have always used canoes. They are a very important part of our culture." —ROKURO MESIAB

Rokuro Mesiab.
Video still by Sea Studios.

Everyone uses canoes

The only thing we had were canoes. That's why they're very important for us. We use them to go fishing. We use them when we go gather coconuts, breadfruit, or taro from other islands, or from another part of the island.

Opposite:
Micronesian canoe model. *Burke Museum collection. Photograph © 1999 Sam Van Fleet.*

We have big canoes and small canoes. Big canoes are for men. Small canoes are for men and women. Women go out and fish on their own. They get together to socialize. Each family has its own canoes. Even children have theirs. Children get together and go fishing and, whether or not they catch any fish, they enjoy it. That's how they practice and learn responsibility. Every child should have a small canoe. As

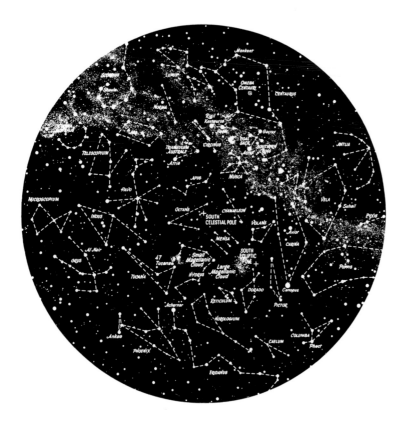

Night sky with stars. *From Will Kyselka,* An Ocean in Mind *(Honolulu: University of Hawai'i Press, 1987).*

tree is enough for one big canoe. There are special ways to learn about building a sailing canoe. It has to be perfect.

Only certain families know the tradition for making sailing canoes and navigating them. They pass on the secret knowledge to a chosen boy in their family. That's the father's job. He's the one who observes and says, "Well, among all my six kids, this one should learn how to build a sailing canoe." He then teaches every secret about sailing canoes to this boy. They start learning when they're young. We have two terms: *rongochik* (RONG-go-chik), a person who listens to every detail of advice from parents and others, and *rongolap* (RONG-go-lap), a person who does not listen to advice. *Rongochik*, a son who listens carefully and hangs around with his father all the time, has the enthusiasm, curiosity, and interest that is needed to learn. That's how he's picked.

I was picked. I was seven years old, the youngest of six boys. People believe that the youngest

they grow up, they have bigger canoes, and when they become adults they have sailing canoes. It's required for all men to know how to sail. That's how they know they are men.

When we come home from a trip, people cook certain kinds of food and put it on the canoe to welcome the canoe home. They celebrate the homecoming canoe by putting flower necklaces on it.

Making and navigating canoes

Canoes are built from breadfruit trees, which are huge. We use men's arms to measure: the circumference of a tree can get as large as three or four men holding their arms together. One

Micronesian canoe. *Photograph courtesy of William Alkire.*

can keep the knowledge for the next generation. In learning, we have to go through a test to prove how strong we are at keeping information to ourselves. We can't be showing off and telling everybody what we know. We learn it and keep it to ourselves. There's a power that comes with it. And with each stage there's medicine, consisting of spells and herbs, that comes with it. At the end, when we pass, we get all the medicine put on our bodies. It blocks curses from others. And that power protects us, no matter what people may try to do. We might not understand it at the time, but it's a very powerful thing.

During the entire time we are making and sailing canoes, we need to follow special customs. For example, we need to ask permission to sail. If a group of young men decides to sail to another island, they have to gather some vegetables, fish, and valuables and go to the sailing master and ask permission to leave. If the master says, "Go ahead, enjoy your trip," it means they can go on their trip and will come back safely. If they sail without asking his permission to leave, their canoe might break down or meet a typhoon on the way.

Child learning navigation, 1983. *Photograph by Stephen Thomas.*

When I started my training, there was a family gathering the first night (I learned at night) to make sure the whole family knew. Of course, my uncle was with me. He had to make sure I understood. Some women wove a big mat from

❁ BEAUTY OF THE NIGHT AND THE MORNING ❁

"Imagine being on a canoe at night under the dark sky and the bright stars. You can't see any land, just dark water all around you. You sit with other men in the canoe. It's very quiet except for some talk every now and then. Alongside the canoe, water moves past as you paddle. Your whole world is that canoe and the sky and stars above it and the water around it. Imagine yourself in the morning waking up in the canoe. You open your eyes to a beautiful sunrise. You see birds leaving home in search of fish, and dolphins playing in the distance. You want to play with them, so you call them by whistling or tapping on a piece of metal underwater. They jump and change their course to come to you. Schools of small fish leap up together, splashing silver patterns on the surface of the water as their scales shine in the sun. You keep on paddling. When the paddle breaks the water, it sounds like music. There's a beauty of the night. And there's a beauty of the morning."—ROKURO MESIAB

Pacific Islanders were the most daring deep-sea voyagers the world has ever known. Between 3,000 and 4,000 years ago, in double-hulled canoes built with stone tools, they sailed by stages from Southeast Asia across the Pacific, the world's largest and deepest ocean. This was centuries before the Vikings plied the coasts of Europe in comparatively short voyages, or before Columbus crossed the Atlantic. The navigational challenges involved in reaching the small and scattered Pacific Islands explains, in part, why this was the last region of the world to be settled by humans. Transporting their domestic animals and vegetables with them, Pacific Islanders eventually settled virtually every habitable island across the vast ocean.

Traveling the Pacific in a Tahitian double-hulled canoe (*pahi*).
Painting © 1988 Herb Kawainui Kane.

the leaves of a pandanus tree. My uncle had some rocks and laid them down on the mat. The mat represented the sky. He pointed out north, east, south, west, and the equator. He used rocks to illustrate, saying that in January the sun would be here, the moon would be there, and this star would be right here. And, as the night went by, the sun would go in this direction, the moon would be right here, and the star that you use would be right there. Each star represents a location, and there are many stars. If we go to one island, we use a particular star to guide us. As the night goes by, new stars come up and the sky changes.

Well, the question somebody is going to ask is, "What if it rains and there are no stars?" It doesn't matter, because we also use other signs when we navigate. We know the wind comes from the north or east. Wherever it comes from, we remember how it hits the canoe. And the wave that we use—we call it *no-lapalap* (noh-LAP-ah-lap)—is a main wave caused by the earth's movement. This wave never changes.

We also learn the migrations of birds. If we get lost and forget where we are, we observe the birds. Micronesians say that birds always know what time they're supposed to be somewhere. Early in the morning, birds leave the island to go fishing. They fish all day, and when they're full, guess what? They go home! So we follow them and say, "Oh, that must be the island." Each island, each group of islands, has certain birds that live there. We memorize all of this. The fish, the whales, even turtles. Turtles have a home. They have a path they follow from the shore. They go out as far as they can and they go back home. We learn that, too.

Learning by listening and doing

We are very, very respectful of people with navigational knowledge. When they are present, we don't walk near them. When they sit down, we sit down. When they talk, we are quiet and listen. That's how we learn, and how we learn to talk. We listen to the respected people talking. They talk and are very careful about what they say. Everything they say has a deeper meaning to it. That's how we learn.

When we make canoes and learn navigation skills, we learn important values about our traditions. The difference between learning in Micronesia and learning in the United States is that in Micronesia we learn by doing. It's not lecture-style only. We don't have a lecture in one class and then go to a lab and have a different professor. In Micronesia, we have one teacher we stick with the whole time. We can learn other things from other people. But we learn navigation knowledge from only one source, our family—our mother and father, and our uncles and aunts—because their advice is the correct advice for our particular family. They teach us.

When we learn navigation from our family, we are learning not only about building a canoe but about our whole system of respect and about hierarchy within the family. We learn this from whatever we do. If we build a canoe, we learn who gets the greatest respect, and next on down the line, as well as how to build the canoe. When we finish building the canoe, we have a celebration. We know who gets which kind of food, who gets served first, and next on down the line. Everything has a hierarchy. That's one value that we teach, respect for our family. That's

Learning by doing: gathering fish in the lagoon at low tide, Eauripik, 1989. *Photograph by David Hawelmai.*

our government. Culture is a set of laws. We don't have an executive, legislative, and judiciary branch. Ours are all combined. Parents are the executive, the legislative, and the judiciary. They make rules, they enforce them, and they punish us. And do we follow their rules? We'd better, because everybody is following them.

Motor boats replace canoes at a cost

You can see the changes and how much outside influence is coming in. Now, back home, some people use boats with engines and put their canoes in storage. Those who have money start buying American boats or start building their own. Yet children still learn in the same way. When a father builds a boat, all the kids sit there and help him build it. Then they start building their own small boats. When they grow bigger, their boats get bigger. Boats, in general, are getting bigger. Before, engines started with six or ten horsepower, but now they go to two hundred. And now a family might have two or more boats. It seems like a requirement now for every man to have his own boat rather than a canoe.

But there aren't many advantages to modern boats. Not everyone can repair the engine when it breaks down. If there are no tools or extra spark plugs, we're in trouble. If we run out of gas, that's a problem. If the motor breaks, that's a problem. With a canoe, if part of it breaks, we can repair it with rope and continue sailing. If a canoe capsizes, we know a technique to turn it right side up. A canoe can float for weeks until people find you. But that's not true with a boat.

If the boat sinks, it's gone. The engine is so heavy that it sinks the boat.

Also, women don't use boats. With canoes, women could get together, go on their own, and spend days and days on the small islands, socializing, doing their own thing. Husbands stayed home and took care of the house. But women don't do that in boats. They're not interested in learning how to be mechanics and repair engines.

Boats are valued too highly to be wasted, because everything on a boat has to be purchased—wood, nails, the engine, gas, everything. So we have to be careful about it. But with a canoe, hey, we have millions of trees. We can cut down a tree and build a canoe for free. If we break it, so what, we can build another one.

Losing family unity in America

I wish there were a program to teach our children about the way we used to live. We didn't have any electricity, but we enjoyed life. I remember

Motor boats are common now: cleaning the boat after a fishing trip, Eauripik, 1994. *Photograph by David Hawelmai.*

❊ LEARNING FROM THE MASTERS IN NEW WAYS ❊

"In Micronesia, we learned while we were growing up. When we were small, we'd hang around older people when they were making canoes so that we could help out. When I was about ten years old, I worked with older men or was around them if they needed any help. When somebody was making a canoe, everybody went to help. But only one person was in charge of making it. We had to follow what he said. When I was back home visiting Eauripik Island some years ago, I saw more outboard motors. But they're starting to make more canoes now, too. They're trying to go back to the old ways. The knowledge used to be passed down by clans or families. Now young men are being taught by one or two people in a classroom environment."
—DAVID HAWELMAI

my life; it was paradise. There was no such thing as being worried about food, money, or clothing. We just got up in the morning and enjoyed life every day. Today it's not the same.

This new life affects family unity. Now money starts separating the family. It's very scary, because money can split a family apart. Before, when we came back from fishing, we divided the fish among our neighbors. Now, because food costs money, people start saying, "The fish are just for us." A husband and wife used to share their money. But now it's "yours" and "mine." It's very scary.

I'm very Americanized and have started to think like an American. I never knew there was such a thing as stress. Now I know that word very well. I'm worried about this, worried about that, the bills and the children.

I have two children, and my children don't listen to me. I want to teach them how to build canoes, build houses, and grow their own vegetables. But they go visit their friends and hang out there and they don't listen to me. They really don't know how to listen.

Here people pay to go to counseling. When I was young, we got counsel from our parents when we ate. That's when we learned—when we ate—because we were a family and my mom and dad talked to the children. We enjoyed listening. I loved to listen to them telling us stories, telling me what was good for me, so I would be respected by others. I would be treated well because I knew right from wrong. I miss that, families being together. Here there isn't the same kind of family unity as there was in our traditional culture.

The value of listening

Learning about navigation is about learning to listen and learning respect. That's very important. We listen to every single thing navigation masters say, and to the way they present things to us. They explain a concept by telling a story about it. They illustrate the quality of life in the lesson. They tell us why it's important to learn about canoes and navigation—because otherwise we'd get lost! They tell us the story about the person who got lost because he didn't listen. He looked back and said, "Uh-oh, what did they say I should do when something like this happens?" But the one who listened knew, "Oh, when that happens, this is what I should do." And that's extremely important. That's why we enjoy listening to other people talking. We can sit for hours and hours. I get together with my Micronesian friends in Seattle and we talk about what's going on here, what's in the newspaper, and what's on TV. We also get together for small church services in each other's houses. We listen to one another.

Missing canoes

In the United States I can't act like a Micronesian, because I'd look strange to other people. I wouldn't survive. When I'd get my paycheck, I'd buy food for everybody. Then I'd run out of money. When Micronesians get paid, they come home and say, "What food do we need?" Then they go and buy enough for everybody. They could spend their whole paycheck just to make sure they got enough food for everybody. The next person would come and say, "When we run out of food again, I'll go buy food for everybody." But now, since we're here, we have to live like Americans and budget for ourselves only. "This is for me, nothing for you. If you're my roommate, too bad. You buy your own food, I'll buy mine."

Hokule'a sailing from Seattle to San Francisco, July 1995. *Photograph by David Brown.*

When I first came here in 1980, I lived in Michigan. The first summer, I bought food for all six people in my apartment. Every day I cooked for six people, and they enjoyed eating it! Then one of them pulled me aside and said, "Rocky, we don't do that. Everybody has their own money; they feed themselves." I said, "I wondered why I've been waiting for you to cook for all of us. When I come home each day,

✸ A VOYAGING RENAISSANCE ACROSS THE PACIFIC ✸

Early Polynesians built and sailed double-hulled, oceangoing canoes. But this skill began to dissipate soon after the arrival of the first Europeans in the late 1700s, and within a century had disappeared from memory. In the 1970s, the Polynesian Voyaging Society was founded in Hawai'i to increase knowledge about early settlement of the Pacific. The goal was to create a vessel similar to the ancient voyaging

canoe and to sail it from Hawai'i to Tahiti and back, guided by the wind, waves, birds, and stars. The Hokule'a (HOH-koo-LAY-ah), a 61-foot double-hulled canoe, was built according to ancient knowledge and made the voyage without modern navigational instruments. This achievement marked the beginning of a voyaging renaissance throughout Polynesia and in Micronesia as well.

Nainoa Thompson, a man of Hawaiian descent who lives in Honolulu, was the navigator of the Hokule'a on its 6,000-mile course. Nainoa could no longer learn from his family but needed a teacher in order to acquire navigational knowledge. For this he turned to Mau Piailug, a Micronesian man who still knew the skills taught by his ancestors.

"I miss going on canoes. It's fun to go sailing in a canoe, where all you need is wind to get from place to place. I miss making them, especially the big ones. It's fun to work on them. I've been trying to get my dad, who is living with us now in Tacoma, to build a canoe so we could use it in Puget Sound. It would probably take four months or so to build. It would be an outrigger, but probably not very big, maybe just 10 feet, because it would be hard to move it around here if it's too big. I think it would be the first Micronesian canoe to be built in the United States. I want to do this to brush up. It's been more than twenty years since I've built a canoe, so I'm kind of rusty. I want to practice so I don't forget how. We'd build it the same way they do on Yap, in Micronesia. I've forgotten some of the names of the canoe parts. I need to make one so my father can tell me the names. I'd make my kids help. We'd get some other people to help, too. I don't want to forget how to make canoes."—DAVID HAWELMAI

you've already eaten your sandwich. But when I cook, I cook for everybody." So he said, "You don't feed everybody. You only buy enough for yourself." I was lucky that he explained that this is how you do it in the United States.

Our children born in this society are Americanized. Do they like it if we talk to them about the way we were? About sharing and feeding one another? No, they don't. They say, "My sister's money is her money. My money is my money! If she's broke, she can borrow from me, and pay me back plus interest."

I miss canoes. I really, really miss them.

David Hawelmai (right) with his uncle, John Taflelig (left), and his father, Louis Olerag (center), Tacoma, 1995. *Photograph courtesy of David Hawelmai.*

"I have four children. I send them over to Micronesia for several months at a time to learn the language and pick up some of the culture. This is my daughter, Roxana Hawelmai [far right], and friends on Eauripik, 1997" (David Hawelmai). *Photograph courtesy of David Hawelmai.*

6 **VIETNAMESE INCENSE BURNER**

Vehicle for Carrying Prayers

ROSE DANG and THUY VU

"The incense burner provides a way for people to communicate with the dead. It's the means to bridge the gap between earth and heaven—between the living and the deceased. When incense sticks are burned, the smoke carries our prayers to the ancestors."—ROSE DANG

Cult of the ancestors

We Vietnamese take ancestor worship very seriously. Filial piety is our duty. When we set a good example for our children, we show respect

Opposite:
Incense burner. *Burke Museum collection. Photograph © 1999 Sam Van Fleet.*

Rose Dang. *Photograph © 2000 Mary Randlett.*
Thuy Vu. *Photograph © 2000 Mary Randlett.*

❀ EXAMPLES OF FILIAL PIETY ❀

1 To warm his father's bed in winter, Hoang Huong lay in it for hours before his father came to bed.

2 Ngo Manh was only eight, but he knew how to protect his parents from mosquito bites. Being too poor to buy mosquito netting, he lay motionless in bed with his shirt off, inviting the mosquitoes to feast on him and spare his parents.

3 Duong Huong accompanied his father to a nearby village. A tiger suddenly jumped out of a bush to attack his father. With a small knife, the boy bravely fought the tiger off, saving his father's life.

Examples of filial piety sketched from the Burke Museum's inlaid cabinet, 2005. *Burke Museum collection. Illustrations by Arn Slettebak.*

for our parents and carry on the tradition. The cult of the ancestors is very, very old. Ancestors are believed to maintain a strong interest in the well-being of their descendants. They provide protection and guidance, but also may cause misfortune if disrespected. Many Vietnamese consider the cult of the ancestors to be their prime religion. The obligations of filial piety require that sons respect their ancestors. This has its roots in Confucianism, which reinforces respect of elders as the source of one's life and social standing. The living are duty-bound to honor their ancestors long after death through prayers, offerings, and consultation.

"Our family is Buddhist, but at the same time, we follow the cult of the ancestors. We had two separate altars when I was growing up—one dedicated to Buddha and the religion, which my grandmother took care of, and another one dedicated to our family ancestors, which my grandfather took care of. We still do this in America. My mother has one altar for the Buddha, and another altar for the ancestors."—THUY VU

The majority of people in Vietnam are Buddhist; some are Christian. They worship in temples and in churches. In the villages, people also believe they need protection from evil spirits and believe in protectors of the villages. They go to communal houses or temples to worship their gods and pray for good crops. All of this is different from ancestor worship in the home.

"At home, we worship our ancestors. Ancestor worship is *the* true religion for all Vietnamese people. We honor the spirits of the ancestors with sincerity and without superstition. Ancestors are respected as

Ancestor worship in a North Vietnamese village.
Photograph © 1996 Ethnic Cultures Publishing House, Hanoi.

❉ RELIGION IN VIETNAM ❉

Numerous religious beliefs coexist in Vietnam, reflecting a commingling of traditions that stems from the country's long history of contact with outsiders. Buddhism is the dominant religion in Vietnam today, although Christianity, Islam, and other sects such as Hoa Hao and Caodaism also have a presence.

Religious freedom has not always been tolerated, and Christians have been persecuted for their beliefs. Today, about 10 percent of the population is Catholic, stemming from the missionizing efforts of Europeans in the sixteenth century. The majority of Catholics presently live around Ho Chi Minh City

(formerly Saigon), to which they fled after the communists took power in the north. Confucianism, which emphasizes duty, courtesy, and virtue, also exerts a strong influence in Vietnam, reinforcing respect for ancestors, elders, and teachers.

On a large altar, the incense burner is flanked on each side by candles. There are typically three small cups for tea or rice wine, three offering bowls, a vase of fresh flowers, and a platter with fruit. Photographs of recently deceased ancestors may be hung above the cabinet. The arrangement of items in twos and threes is symbolic of the yin and yang of the universe and the interconnection between heaven, earth, and human beings. The offerings are often fragrant—families prepare their ancestors' favorite foods on special occasions and fresh tea is offered every day. The smoke from the burning incense carries the family's prayers upward and fills the house or pagoda with a distinctive aroma.

Ancestor altar in a Ngai village home, North Vietnam.
Photograph © 1996 Ethnic Cultures Publishing House, Hanoi.

the source of one's life and social standing. We believe we have a duty to honor our parents and ancestors long after their death, through prayers and offerings and by leading respectable and successful lives. Deceased ancestors remain active family members, providing protection, guidance, and blessings. As in life, so in death parents command respect and obedience. The cult of the ancestors has great social significance for the family and is the tie that binds its members together. It exerts a profound influence on the daily life of the Vietnamese."—ROSE DANG

Ancestor altars at the center of family life

In every traditional family, the ancestral altar (*bàn thờ ông bà*) (bahn tuh ohng bah) is the center of family life. The incense burner (*bát nhang*) (baht nahn) on the altar plays a very important role. Not only on the ancestral altar at home but at the pagoda temple at the Buddhist church and at community events—everywhere—the incense burner is the vehicle that carries one's prayers to whomever one wants to communicate with.

Ancestor altars vary a lot among different families in Vietnam. Poor families in rural areas might have just one simple shelf against the wall, with only one item on the shelf—the incense burner. Others might have stone or wooden stands in their front yards. Wealthy families living in the urban areas can have quite sophisticated ancestral altars. But no matter how simple or complex, the incense burner is the one item that should not be absent from any family altar.

Inviting the ancestors home

Every year, the anniversary of the death of an ancestor is a big event and all the family ancestors are invited to come home for a visit. Using the incense shows our respect and conveys our prayers. The altar is the special place to which they come. Just as kings have their thrones, ancestors have their altars. Offering the special food they used to enjoy is our way of showing that we respect and treat our ancestors the same way we did when they were alive. The head of the household (the father or oldest son) stands in front of the altar to invite them, using special wording and prayers to address them. It's a formal, sincere, and solemn invitation. The altar is also a place where we consult the ancestors and seek their spiritual guidance before all major family and business decisions.

"I remember when my brother took the national entrance exam to medical school. The exam was highly competitive and the selection process was very tough. I remember my grandfather in front of the altar, praying for spiritual support and guidance for my brother. My brother needed all the help he could get!"—THUY VU

The ancestors are welcome any time. The ancestral altar is like their home, their special place in the family. But if we want them to be there at a special time, then we need to burn incense and invite them.

"If we burn incense every day, pretty soon the burner is full of incense stubs. Sometimes these stubs just happen to catch fire on their own. It is also a common belief that if we ask our ancestors something and the incense burner catches fire after we have finished, that's a sign that they have heard our calls and appreciate our consulting them. Also, it's a sign that something of importance will be happening in the family. I remember both my grandfather and

Wedding engagement ceremony in front of the family altar.
Photographs courtesy of Rose Dang.

grandmother saying, 'The incense burner caught fire last night. Be prepared. Something of importance might happen in the family.' Sometimes it turned out to be true!"—THUY VU

Burning incense at a Buddhist temple in Cholon, South Vietnam. *Photograph © 1996 Ethnic Cultures Publishing House, Hanoi.*

A variety of shapes and styles

Incense burners come in different shapes, sizes, styles, and materials. Some incense burners are small and just for incense sticks. Others, usually made of brass or ceramic, with a lid, can hold incense cones. Some are very large, like the ones found at a Buddhist temple or pagoda. Because of the large number of people visiting a temple, the incense sticks have to be burned outside. Others, like those seen in the courtyard of the royal tomb in Hue (whey) in central Vietnam, are called urns and are symbols of royalty.

The different types of incense burners are used for different purposes. We burn the incense sticks every day and the cones on special occasions—like the anniversary of the death of an ancestor, the Lunar New Year, or a wedding. When we cover the burners, the smoke comes out slowly and curls up in different directions, instead of just going straight up. The large incense sticks are used for decorations in the home.

An incense burner can also be used as decoration during a special event, like a musical performance in the home. This is not the same incense burner as the one we have on the altar. That one must be there all the time. We cannot just pull it from the cabinet and place it on the table or on the floor in the middle of the circle of people listening to the music!

"The incense burner has special meaning to people, and we are supposed to take good care of it. If we go to somebody's house and break the incense burner, that's a very serious offense."—THUY VU

Royal urns as symbols of the dynasty

Whether the incense burner is on the family altar, at the church, or at the king's palace, it also represents the king. That is why the big royal urns look exactly like an incense burner with two handles and three legs. They are symbols of the entire dynasty—the king, the hero of the people—and represent pride in the history of the nation. This is part of the reason why the incense burner plays such a very important role in the life of the people in Vietnam.

The nine urns in front of the dynastic temple in Hue represent the nine Nguyen kings. In the royal tomb, there is an altar for the king. In front of the picture of the king is the three-legged, covered incense burner used with cones. There is another one on the floor for incense sticks. We can tell this is the king's altar because of the large size and the red and gold colors. These are symbols of royalty. No matter how wealthy they are, common families cannot use these colors or the designs of the dragons and the phoenix.

Tablets carry the names of the ancestors

The throne (*khảm thờ*) (kahm tuh) and ancestor tablets (*bài vị*) (bye vee) are also key components of the family altar, along with the incense burner. The throne sits on the altar cabinet and the incense burner is placed in front of the throne. The ancestor tablet is kept on the throne. The tablet holds the names of the ancestors. It shows the continuation of the generations, where people belong in a family. The tablets carry the names, birth dates, and sometimes show the lineage of the ancestors—what family the tablets belong to. They are made out of bamboo or wood. They can be purchased, or you can make them yourself. But you need to write the names of your ancestors yourself. The size depends on the size of the *khảm thờ*, because it has to fit inside. Each ancestor has a separate tablet. In some families, the *khảm thờ* has a small curtain in front. In special ceremonies, the curtain is opened to invite the ancestors home. At the end of the day, after the end of the anniversary, the curtain is closed.

Vu family altar with tablets and urns. *Photograph © 2000 Mary Randlett.*

The history of Vietnam has been marked by centuries of invasions, revolts, and reconquests. Ancestors of today's population first appeared in the region more than 4,000 years ago. Around 100 B.C., Chinese invaded from the north and maintained control over the area for more than 1,000 years. While China ruled in the north, two separate kingdoms grew in the south—the Champa kingdom in the central zone, and the Khmer empire farther south. In 938 A.D., the Chinese were defeated by the Viet people, and there followed nine centuries of independent rule by a succession of royal families. These dynasties withstood periodic attacks and incursions from neighboring armies and managed to expand their territory southward.

From the 1500s onward, European traders and missionaries were also present in Vietnam. The French colonized and ruled from 1867 to 1954. Following World War II, Western fears of the spread of communism led to U.S. military involvement in Southeast Asia.

In 1954, Vietnam was divided at the 17th parallel and communist rule was established in the north. Subsequent efforts to reunite the country failed and civil war broke out, leading to the Vietnam War. In April 1975, Saigon fell to the North and thousands of South Vietnamese fled the country, many coming to the United States as war refugees. Today, there are more than 18,000 Vietnamese Americans living in Washington State.

Carrying on ancestor worship in America

"I come from a very traditional family. The worship of the ancestors is something we have to carry on. We have to pass it down to the younger generations. At my home, the anniversary of the death of my mother, my father, my mother-in-law, or my father-in-law is a chance for my husband and me to remind the children of our ancestors, our parents, and our obligations to carry on the family history and values. We burn incense, make offerings, say prayers, and practice the obligations of filial piety. We want our children to carry on these traditions."—ROSE DANG

Vietnamese ancestor-worship traditions were brought to America after the collapse of South Vietnam in 1975. It is very common for Vietnamese American families to have a traditional altar for their ancestors in their homes. But because of all the changes due to living in America, many people have simplified their traditional practices.

Even if things are simplified, a small, decent place is still reserved for the family altar.

Most people put the *khảm thờ*, the *bài vị*, and *bát nhang* on a shelf, either because they cannot afford a big cabinet, or because space is limited. Now that photographs are available, people also often hang pictures of their ancestors above the altar. The presence of the deceased, seen in the pictures, is a constant reminder of family history, values, and traditions. The tablets are still important, too, because they identify the ancestors.

Another change in America is that when the remains of the ancestor are cremated instead of buried, the ash may be put in a small urn on the home altar, or on the altar at a Buddhist temple. For many families, the way the ancestors are summoned has become simplified, too. Now they might just stand in front of the altar and say what they have on their minds, rather than phrasing it in a formal way. Others carry on the practices in a more traditional manner.

"It's not easy keeping the language and culture alive here. It has been more than twenty years for us. A lot of parents have given up because they think that sooner or later they'll lose everything anyway—the language, the tradition. We don't want to give up. It's not just our family, but other families, too. It's a difficult task, both for us and for the children. When the children are home, they have to be traditional,

Dang family altar flanked by dragons. *Photograph © 2000 Mary Randlett.*

respectful, and obedient. When they go out, they have to be progressive, strong. The differences sometimes cause confusion for the young generation if the roots and the wings provided by the parents are not strong enough."—ROSE DANG

❋ DRAGONS ❋

Dragons are frequently placed on or above ancestral altars. They are ancient symbols of good luck and fortune and are said to be the first ancestors of all Vietnamese people. Legends tell of a lonely dragon from China that wandered south to what is now Vietnam. This dragon was personified as a man who married the dragon lord's daughter, producing a son, who became the first king of Vietnam. This king taught his people many things, including how to till the soil, sow seed, and prepare foods. He eventually married an immortal princess, and all Vietnamese are said to be descended from their union.

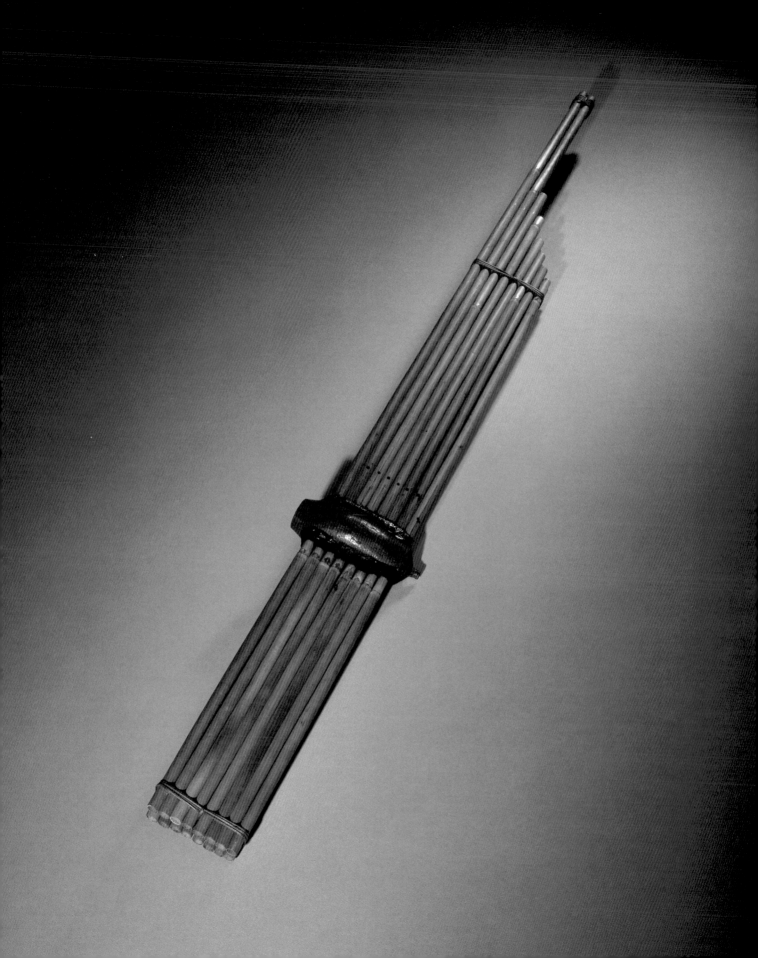

7 LAO *KHAEN*

Instrument of Spiritual Nourishment

KHAMPHA CHANTHARANGSY, with KHAM OUI SIKHANTHAT

"For me, the khaen *is the same as Lao identity. When I see or hear the word* khaen, *or when you ask me about it, I see the* khaen *representing Lao culture and Lao people. Wherever you find* khaen, *Lao people exist. Even in northeast Thailand or in southern China, if people play the* khaen, *then they are Lao. Lao people went to the United States and to other countries in the world. Anywhere you go, if people play the* khaen, *they came from Laos."*

—KHAM OUI SIKHANTHAT

"When I look at the khaen, *it's as if I see a parrot who can talk my language. I don't see it as an instrument. I see it as alive. It has life, just like a parrot that you train, a parrot that you talk to in your language."*

—KHAMPHA CHANTHARANGSY

Opposite:
Khaen. *Burke Museum collection. Photograph © 1999 Sam Van Fleet.*

Khampha Chantharangsy (left) playing the *khaen* **with Kham Oui Sikanthat (right).** *Photograph © 2000 Mary Randlett.*

Khampha Chantharangsy with a *khaen*. Photograph © 2000
Mary Randlett.

My *khaen* comforts me

I was born and lived in the countryside of Laos,
and I never saw anything that was as important
to my life as the *khaen* (kan). It's like spiritual
nourishment, not just for me but for many people. When people are sick, others play the *khaen*
to comfort them and make them feel better.

The *khaen* made me cry many times because
of its sound and the meaning of the songs.
They are kind of sad. That's part of the difference between Eastern and Western culture.
Most of our literature ends with sadness, to
make people sympathize with someone or
something and cry. Whoever writes something
that touches someone's heart, who gets tears
out of someone, that's the best writer.

Throughout my life, which went up and
down and up and down, there were many times
that sadness would come, like from a war, or
missing family members or friends. Then when
I heard the sound of the *khaen*, it reminded me
right away of that quality of being Lao. That's
what I strongly believe about the *khaen*. Its
sound has a magical power that sends strong,
meaningful messages to Lao people. No matter where we are or what we do, that quality of
being Lao—unity, honesty, productivity, love,
caring, sharing—should always be remembered
and kept alive.

When I first came to Seattle, I told my wife
that I didn't want anything else but my *khaen*.
I brought my *khaen* with me when I came as a

✺ A CLASSICAL INSTRUMENT ✺

Khaen, the Lao classical instrument,
means "to comfort" or "to lift up
the spirit." It's made of bamboo
pipes, each with a tiny air hole, that
are held together in a hardwood
frame that is sealed with black
beeswax. There are different kinds
of *khaen*. Each has a different quality, depending on the reed, the little
silver or brass tongue inserted inside;
silver is the highest quality. *Khaen*
were sometimes up to ten feet long,
but often they are smaller now
because, as Khampha Chantharangsy says, it's hard, for instance,
to take a really big *khaen* on a bus.

Present-day Laos, a country that historically was never one cohesive entity, is the homeland of people who have experienced a long history of loss. In 1778, during the war with Siam (now Thailand), the capital city, Vientiane, was burned. Lao citizens were made slaves, and their property, gold, and jewelry were confiscated. The best musicians and dancers were sent to serve in the palace in Bangkok. Lao instruments, music, and dancing styles fell into the hands of Thai patrons, who transformed Lao art to please the Siamese. In the late 1800s, French colonization further transformed the region. Lao territory was divided into two areas, each on a different side of the Mekong River. The French popularized Western culture, repressing the art and culture of Laos, substituting the sound of the *khaen* with that of the guitar, accordion, violin, and trumpet.

refugee in 1980, and I got stopped many times at the airport because it looks suspicious. They asked me lots of questions about what it was for. They thought it looked strange. They asked, "What do you have in there?" They couldn't see it because I had it in a case. They thought it was a gun. When they lifted it up, though, they realized a gun wouldn't be that light. Then they opened it up and saw the black beeswax that holds the bamboo pipes together, and were suspicious. Also, I had put a kind of white powder inside to keep it from cracking and they thought that was opium. They asked a lot of questions. Then they let me go. I feel proud that I was able to bring my *khaen* with me, not only to play but also to look at. It brings up my past memories a lot.

I didn't learn to play the *khaen* in Laos. If I were still back home, I wouldn't have learned because there are many excellent *khaen* players and I'd feel frustrated with my skills. I started playing the *khaen* when I was in India. I went to India as a student in 1971 and lived there for five years. I brought my *khaen* with me. I learned to play more when I came to the United States in 1980. Because no one plays for me here, I have to play and listen to myself. My *khaen* can make me cry and comfort me even if I play it myself. When we were at Central Washington University together, Mr. Kham Oui saw that I played it all the time. During those two periods in my life, when I was in India and when I came to Seattle, my *khaen* comforted me.

I have seven *khaen* now. My wife asks me, "Why do you buy lots of *khaen*?" They are

The many *khaen* in Mr. Khampha's house. *Photograph © 2000 Mary Randlett.*

During the Vietnam War, the U.S. military fought in Laos as well as in Vietnam. Fighting alongside their American allies, the Lao tried to close off the Ho Chi Minh Trail, a transport route used by North Vietnamese troops. In this way they hoped to prevent the Pathet Lao, an organization of Lao communists, from seizing control. By 1970, American planes had bombed more than two-thirds of Laos, disrupting the Lao rural economy and forcing many Lao to become refugees. When the war ended in 1975, the Pathet Lao came to power, causing even more Lao to flee their homes. Thousands of Lao lived in refugee camps in Thailand, sometimes for several years. Many were eventually given refuge in the United States in the late '70s and early '80s. For many Lao people, memory is all that remains of their homeland.

expensive. You can get *khaen* from Thailand or in many stores in Seattle. But the question is the quality. You want the best. The *khaen* is like coffee; you want to drink coffee from Starbucks! That's why I have so many *khaen* at home. The first *khaen* I brought with me, and I played it until it got old and the quality deteriorated. Then my wife's sister came to the United States and brought several *khaen* to sell. I bought two from her, so I had three. And then the fourth *khaen* I got from my brother-in-law. The fifth *khaen* I bought down by the Seattle waterfront, at the Pike Place Market, because it was cheap, about twenty-five dollars. But it's not good quality. It's made as a commercial item and it's hard to play. The sixth one is from my sister. Even when I had six *khaen*, I was not happy with any of them. Last year my aunt went back to Laos and I said, "Could you ask Lao people in Laos, not in Thailand, to make a *khaen* for me?" She said yes. When she brought that to me it was the worst! It's hard to blow in and out with it. With the best-quality *khaen* I don't have to use wind that much; if I blow in and out, I feel like elastic. That's the reason I have so many *khaen*.

In Seattle, it's not a good idea to leave the *khaen* out if you really want to play it. I made cases for some of mine so the weather would not affect them that much. In the winter when it's cold and I turn on the heat, that's bad. If I lay the *khaen* down flat, the reed inside bends down and that makes it hard to play. When I play, I adjust it. I can use a butter knife or the end of a barbecue stick to tighten the wax inside. And then, every week, if I don't forget, I take them out and press the beeswax. It needs to be pressed very often, otherwise it will harden. And after I'm done playing, I always take a small sip of whiskey and blow into the *khaen*, shake them, and then let them sit and dry. Blowing a little bit of alcohol inside makes it softer, or maybe opens it up a little bit. But it makes a difference. That's the way I take good care of my *khaen*. But it's hard to do that for seven *khaen*.

In Laos, this instrument is not as popular in the city as in the countryside. City people consider it backward. The children in the city don't play the *khaen*. They don't see the value of it because they are Westernized and play guitar or piano. But the *khaen* is very common among the country people. That's why it brings back memories for me. Even when I see a *khaen* in a ten-story building, it always brings me back to my country origins.

Lao lowland countryside. *Photograph courtesy of Songsak Prangwatthanakun.*

I was born in the countryside among poor farmers. But my wife's family was born in the city. Her father was a high-ranking officer, a provincial governor. I see a big difference even now. My wife doesn't have the same feeling I have when I look at the *khaen*. When she hears the sound of the *khaen*, it's not as deep a feeling as it is for me.

The content of songs

Lao people live in the jungle and are touched by the sounds of nature. We play according to what we see and hear in nature, like the song of a bird, the movement of bamboo, or the wave of grain in the field.

We have special kinds of bird songs, espe-cially two kinds. One we call the *noke ka wau* (NOH-keh kah WOW) because the bird sings "ka wau, ka wau." That bird sound matches the sound of the *khaen*, because both sounds are very emotional. They remind us of past memories like death, love, and separation. The other one is called *noke kon dok* (NOH-keh kon DOK) because the bird sings "kon dok, kon dok." Those two kinds of bird songs are meaningful to our lives and make us feel more in tune. If we are crying about something, they make us cry more. And then it brings our memories back.

Sometimes when we have a *khaen*, we sit in the jungle and look up at the branches of the trees, like a bamboo, a very tall bamboo bush. Then, when the wind comes and sways the top of the bamboo, we think, "Oh, that's how I'm going to play the *khaen*." And then we try to play that. And later, when people hear it, they think, "This reminds me of the bamboo, that's what it is." Then they know what song it is.

People can tell whether the music is sad, or funny, or exciting. But it's always relaxing. It makes me feel like a drop on the floor and then I close my eyes. We call that *on xonh* (awn sawn), which means it's not sad but deeply relaxing when we hear the song of the *khaen*.

Songs aren't written. It's not as if this is the song and then we play it. But there are some

Khaen player with seated dancers, 1930s or 1940s. *Photograph by Thomas Renault.*

✿ A SEVEN-TONED OCTAVE ✿

Lao classify musical instruments into four categories: instruments that are plucked, bowed, beaten, and blown. The *khaen*, which is blown, consists of two rows of seven bamboo pipes of different lengths, decreasing in size and arranged in pairs, like two sets of pan pipes placed one on top of the other. The musician blows into the *khaen*, creating the sound as air passes across a vibrating object, usually a brass or silver tongue placed inside the bamboo pipes. Air passes through several pipes at once as the musician steadily breathes in and out, creating a sound that is midway between that of a harmonica and an accordion. Several notes can be played simultaneously and continuously. Lao music has the pitch of a seven-toned octave, corresponding to the scale of a *khaen*.

"You cannot really compare *khaen* music to notes and scales for the Western ear. Many Western people might say that it sounds meaningless or inharmonious. But for us, when we hear the *khaen*, it's melodious."
—KHAM OUI SIKHANTHAT

written songs now. One written song is about a widow who comforts her baby, singing it to sleep without food. When a person hears that, it's very sad. The life of a single mother is not that simple, especially in our country. She has to work in the fields to raise the baby. Another written song for the *khaen*—this one's not sad but funny—is about a dog that runs along the beach and makes the sound "ja ja ja ja." When we hear that song, it makes us think, "Oh, that's right, it's the dog on the beach." An expert *khaen* player can even add the sound by using his tongue. Another written song is about a train on the track. This is very famous. It's modern.

In the United States, people play new songs. But even if we play American or European songs with the *khaen*, we always want to bring the original tune back, because new songs don't mean as much to us in our new world.

Originally, the *khaen* was played by itself or to accompany people singing *lum* (folk songs). There are not many songs where we play the *khaen* alone, without having a singer who sings along. *Khaen* and *lum* are like husband and wife. They can't be separated. *Khaen* and *lum* go together like sticky rice and pickled fish. People won't listen to *khaen* alone for more than an hour or two. But if we play with *lum*, they'll listen from nine o'clock in the evening until four o'clock in the morning. And when we learn *lum*, we don't just learn a song, memorize it, and sing it. To learn *khaen* and *lum* is different than that. They must be learned and played together. Nowadays, there are many modern concerts that use five *khaen* in one concert, or five *khaen* along with modern technology. If you see that, you know it's new.

Learning how to play

The *khaen* depends on a *moh khaen*, or *khaen* player, to make it melodious. Not every person from Laos is able to play. A person might blow into it and play, but won't necessarily make music. It takes practice and also talent. In Laos, we don't have schools to learn how to play the *khaen*.

Originally in Laos, before Buddhism, people believed in spirits. Whenever they wanted to do anything, they always prayed. Even to learn to play the *khaen*, they didn't go to school but went to an older person. If they were learning from somebody, they spent all day, all week, even all month, playing with that person. They took five pairs of candles, five pairs of flowers, and a bottle of alcohol, just to ask to learn to play from that person. They had to follow specific rules, and everything was tied to spirits, in terms of learning the *khaen*. There were certain rules they had to follow. They couldn't walk under clotheslines or under houses—in Laos the houses are raised above the ground. And when they ate, they couldn't let anyone touch their hands or they would have to stop eating. And they couldn't eat pumpkins or squash. There were lots of rules. And there's a special kind of word they had to memorize to lift up their spirits. And then they had to pray and start memorizing to open up their minds.

My goal is not to be professional but just to have fun. If I really wanted to be professional, I would have to meet with the older person, pay the price, and do the ceremony.

Whether they are farmers or city dwellers, Laotians gather at the end of the dry season to celebrate Boun Bang Fai (boon bung fye) (Rocket Festival). They implore Phaya Thaen (PYE-ya tan), Head of the Heavens, to send the monsoon rains to ensure a bountiful rice harvest and prosperity for the community. The festival also commemorates the birth, death, and enlightenment of the Buddha.

The highlight of Boun Bang Fai is the parading and firing of colorful rockets, which represent the mythical water serpent Naga, a symbol of male potency. The rockets are carried to the firing ground in a boisterous parade, enlivened by music, song, and dance. During the parade, using nets and fish traps, men mimic the catching of fish. They make suggestive jokes about

"male" and "female" fish found in the mud of flooded rice fields. Members of Seattle's Lao community have celebrated Boun Bang Fai at the Burke Museum several times, parading the rockets through the University of Washington campus but stopping short of firing them.

Lao Boun Bang Fai parade, University of Washington campus, Seattle, May 1999 (from left to right: Mr. Phaysane, Mr. One, Mr. Songka, Mr. Khampha). *Photograph by Miriam Kahn.*

Above:
Lao Boun Bang Fai parade with three rockets,
University of Washington campus, Seattle, 1995.
Photograph by Su Ratsamee.

Right:
Mr. Thongphan playing cymbals and Mr. One preparing
the fishnet, University of Washington campus,
Seattle, 1995. *Photograph by Su Ratsamee.*

8 PHILIPPINE SANTO NIÑO

Icon of the Holy Child

JACK BUZZARD and MARCELA ANTONIA BUZZARD

*"I was born on exactly the same date as the Fiesta del Santo Niño in Cebu City, the Philippines—
on January 17, 1936. According to my mom, my dad told her that he was going to leave the maternity
ward to go visit the basilica and thank Señor Santo Niño, since everything was fine when my mother
delivered me. Ever since that time, they called me Antonia, for Santo Niño. Even today, every time
I ask for His help, He provides it. He has never failed me."* —MARCELA BUZZARD

Survival of an icon

Santo Niño is the holy image of the Christ
Child. The statuette that became known as
the Santo Niño was brought to the Philippines
by the Spanish explorer Ferdinand Magellan,
who landed on the island of Cebu (SEE-boo) in
1521. The Santo Niño has long been a source of

Opposite:

Santo Niño statue. *Burke Museum collection. Photograph
© 1999 Sam Van Fleet.*

Marcela and Jack Buzzard. *Photograph © 2000 Mary Randlett.*

power for the Cebuanos (SAY-boo-ah-nos), and has spread all over the country. It is now the patron saint of the Philippines.

The Santo Niño is not actually a saint. It is the child Jesus who grew up to be Jesus Christ. The original statuette was from Belgium. It was given to Queen Juana of Cebu by Magellan after she was baptized into the Catholic faith. Magellan had been well taken care of in 1521, and the statuette was symbolic of the successful voyage. But problems soon arose between the conquistadors and the natives, and many were killed, including Magellan. A few of the ships were able to get out and return to Spain.

It was not until 1565 that another Spanish expedition came to Cebu. The leader of the new expedition was Miguel Lopez de Legazpi. He did not have as good a reception as Magellan. There was hostility, and he opened fire and burned the village where Cebu City now stands. One of his soldiers, Juan Camus, went ashore to look at the burned village. He went to a hut that was still standing and found a European pine box. He opened it and there was another box inside. He opened that, too. In it was the original statuette of the Santo Niño! The priest accompanying the expedition, Fra Urdaneta,

said a Thanksgiving Mass. The location of the Basilica Minore del Santo Niño, which was built in the 1700s, is near the site of that burned hut. Since then, there have been many, many testimonials of miracles occurring around the child Jesus. That statuette of the Santo Niño is the oldest religious relic in the country.

Festival of the Holy Child

"Ever since I was born, I remember that during the time of the festivity of Señor Santo Niño, people from all walks of life came and worshipped at the basilica."
—JACK BUZZARD

"Whoever is asking something of Señor Santo Niño—farmers who want a good harvest, or students who want to pass a test, or children who have left the homeland and are not following Filipino tradition and—He will answer their prayers."
—MARCELA BUZZARD

The third week of January is the biggest celebration in the Philippines—the Fiesta del Santo Niño. It has grown in popularity over the past 400 years. What at first was a small procession down to the sea has become a grand parade.

❋ **ORIGIN OF THE STATUE** ❋

The original Santo Niño of Cebu is a small, 14-inch statue of the Christ Child. It was made in Belgium in the early sixteenth century and brought to the Philippines by Ferdinand Magellan in 1521. At that time, Spain was leading efforts to "re-Catholicize" the world after the Reformation and encouraged devo-

tion to the Christ Child as King. In the Philippines, the statue is referred to as Señor Santo Niño to distinguish it from the infant Jesus in the crib. A similar statue, which came to be known as the Holy Infant of Prague, was presented to the friars of Carmel in Prague, Czechoslovakia, in 1628. Replicas of the Prague

statue—which is distinguished from the Santo Niño by its ebony black color—were eventually brought to the Philippines and reside in numerous churches there, as do copies of the original Santo Niño enshrined in the basilica.

❈ *SINULOG* ❈

The *sinulog* is a dance performed to thank the Santo Niño for favors granted and to petition Him with new requests. It has come to be performed in several different ways. The *sinulog* danced by the candle vendors in front of the basilica is a dance of personal supplication that has its roots in an ancient folk form. There are also *sinulog* troupes who reenact scenes from Philippine history, including the arrival of Magellan in Cebu. In 1965, Cebu celebrated the fourth centennial of the Santo Niño's rediscovery by Miguel Lopez de Legazpi, and many of these troupes performed in the celebration. In 1980, a new Sinulog Festival was formed to feature parade competitions of these dance troupes. The Sinulog Festival has continued to grow and is now the central focus of tourism promotions for the Fiesta del Santo Niño. Meanwhile, vendors can still be found selling candles and dancing for patrons in front of the basilica.

Sinulog, **Cebu City, Philippines, 1966.** *Photograph courtesy of Karl L. Hutterer.*

Candle vendor, Cebu City, Philippines, 1966. *Photograph courtesy of Karl L. Hutterer.*

Now almost a million people come. Catholics, Muslims, pilgrims, and tourists come from all parts of the world. During an evening parade, the image of the Holy Child is carried along on a float through the streets of Cebu. People light candles and pray for blessings.

The *sinulog* (SEE-noo-log) is a dance of prayer—an offering of candles and prayers to the Holy Child. It used to be that you bought a candle in front of the basilica and danced. Now, whoever sells the candle says, "I will dance for you and pray for you." So you give them money and then just watch from the side.

❄ *NOVENAS* ❄

Novenas are special prayers that seek help or mediation from particular patron saints. They are typically recited for nine consecutive days, or once a week for nine weeks. *Novena* is also the name of the small prayer book that is used to aid the faithful with their recitations. Although *novenas* have long been used to obtain help from the Holy Child, a perpetual *novena* to the Santo Niño was established in 1958 and has been performed every Friday at the Basilica Minore (formerly the Church of San Agustin) since that time. Individuals may also say *novenas* in front of home altars or in other Catholic churches.

Evening procession, Fiesta del Santo Niño, Cebu City, Philippines, 1966. *Photograph courtesy of Karl L. Hutterer.*

***Novena** prayer booklet. Burke Museum collection. Photograph courtesy of the Burke Museum.*

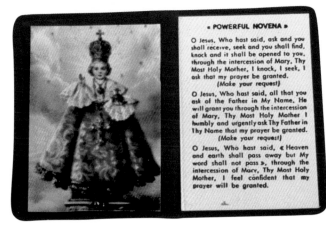

"When I was a youth growing up in Cebu, people in the older generation were the leaders in the Fiesta del Santo Niño. They were the ones who arranged everything. The old ones still do *novenas* [noh-VEE-nahs]

[scripted prayers] to the Santo Niño on Friday nights. The younger ones dance for prayers to continue their studies, or for other things. It is a devotion for all people of all ages."—JACK BUZZARD

"When I was growing up in Cebu, I went to church every Friday and Sunday. My mom and I believed in going to the basilica for prayers. On Fridays, I went to the *novenas*. It would be so crowded that you could not get inside the church. But you could hear the songs. Even inside, you couldn't see the statue because of all the people. Every week! During the fiesta, you couldn't even get close."
—MARCELA BUZZARD

Over the years, the fiesta has grown larger and larger. Since the late 1960s, the religious observations are followed by a Mardi Gras–type celebration, with all kinds of dancing and parades. It has become much more commercialized now. Businesses have floats with signs right on them that say, "This is our business . . . , plus we're sponsoring Fiesta del Santo Niño!"

A gold crown and burgundy cape

The Santo Niño holds a scepter in his right hand and raises two fingers in blessing for peace. The old people say his two raised fingers represent 2,000 years. In his left hand, he holds the world, a sign of Christianity. He also wears a crown, which is always gold, and has a cape with gold sequins. The color of the cape was originally burgundy. There are some today that are green. But the cape is supposed to be burgundy or red, not green. The Chinese people who have department stores in the Philippines have green ones.

They believe that having the Señor Santo Niño in their businesses will bring prosperity.

His original skin color was olive—not dark, but also not white. Many people think it got darkened from the heat when the old village burned. All the Santo Niños that are made and blessed now are made to look dark, like the original after it was darkened.

The modern figures are icons—replicas of the original statuette. Devotees purchase them and bring them to the church to be blessed—to any church, but especially to the basilica. The original Santo Niño is not always out on display anymore. There were times when it was, but it has been threatened. Once it was set on fire, and then, people said, a flash of light occurred. The statue wasn't damaged, but they don't want to take any more chances. Another time, during World War II, the Santo Niño disappeared. They thought that the Japanese military soldiers had taken it, but it came back. They found a lot of stickers on his clothes and the clothes were dirty. Since then, they have had to be more careful with it.

Statues for sale, Cebu City, Philippines, 1966. *Photograph courtesy of Karl L. Hutterer.*

Señor Santo Niño is everywhere

Once you step into Cebu, you see statues and pictures of Señor Santo Niño everywhere. The jeepneys, the limousines, all the transportation—they all have a little statue inside the car. Even in department stores. Here, in America, we don't mix religion and government. In the Philippines, you can go into government offices and see statues of the Santo Niño in the mayor's and other department heads' offices!

"I have a small Santo Niño replica in my mother's old bedroom here in Seattle, and we have a bigger one in our bedroom. A friend of mine has a laundromat, and she has a big one with lights right at the entrance. So we have him here, too, but not in the government offices!"—MARCELA BUZZARD

Bringing Santo Niño to Seattle

An icon of the Santo Niño of Cebu was blessed and enshrined at St. James Cathedral in Seattle in September 1996. For some of the Filipinos living in Seattle, it had been years since they had participated in the public ceremony honoring the image. It was also the first time for many of their children to participate in the tradition.

What we're trying to do in Seattle is to let the Filipinos be aware that there is a Señor Santo Niño here now. They should come and listen to the prayers. We Filipinos, as diverse as we are in language and customs, should band together to celebrate and learn what Santo Niño is all about.

"To establish a chapter for the worship of Santo Niño in Seattle, we had to obtain permission from St. Augustine Church in Philadelphia. I had first asked in Cebu, but was told that it was the people in Philadelphia who were issuing the chapters, because that is the center of devotion for Santo Niño in the United States. When I asked the pastor, he said yes, and that we would be the first in our area to receive permission to establish a chapter. He sent all the papers and bylaws. Once it was approved by the diocesan canon lawyer, the statue could be enshrined. I had gotten a big one in Cebu (about 40 inches tall) and donated it to the church. We've now celebrated the Fiesta del Santo Niño in Seattle since 1996."—JACK BUZZARD

The Santo Niño festival is not as commercial in Seattle as it is in the Philippines. The observances are more subdued. We mostly just do the part in the church. We have a High Mass and a light lunch at the parish hall that is free to anyone who wants to come. There are also events

❋ A LONG HISTORY OF DEVOTION ❋

Devotion to the Santo Niño of Cebu began even before the statue was enshrined. According to early written accounts, local Cebuanos had begun treating the Santo Niño as an idol with special powers shortly after its presentation by Magellan to Queen Juana in 1521. During the forty-four years between the departure of Magellan and the arrival of Legazpi, who found the figure in the burning embers of Cebu, the Santo Niño was credited with many miracles, including restoration of health, protection from enemies, and delivery of rain during drought.

Once it was enshrined, it became a central focus of Catholic devotion on the island of Cebu. After the first Mass held in its honor, those in attendance vowed to celebrate its recovery with an annual feast day, which has come to be known as the Fiesta del Santo Niño.

at the community center, like the festival-style *sinulog*. Although you have to pay admission at the community center, we don't charge anything for the food at the church. That is the old tradition from the Philippines. Not only during Santo Niño but at other town festivals, everyone who comes gets fed.

Prayers still answered

"During World War II, it was so hard in the Philippines. There was no food, no clothing, nothing. One time, we were evacuated far from the city and the fishermen couldn't find any fish. This is what my mom told me. The fishermen had a net, and it was windy. When it's windy and stormy, there are no fish. Then all of a sudden, they saw a little dark boy playing by the water. They didn't know who he was. He said, 'Throw your net over here.' So they threw their net over there and caught some fish! When they tried to find him again, he was gone. My mom said it was true. It was another miracle from Señor Santo Niño! It's still going on."—MARCELA BUZZARD

Since the Santo Niño came to St. James Cathedral, there have been stories of answers to prayers—testimonials that Santo Niño has helped people, restored their health, helped families. One man hadn't been able to walk for two years. The first time we had the Santo Niño at St. James, the man had a handkerchief and he was crying—he wiped it all over Santo Niño's feet and he wiped it on his own feet. Now he's okay! For two years, he thought he was going to die. Now he has boots, he goes to church, and he serves with us in the cathedral. Another family was on the verge of divorce and has been

Father Michael Ryan and Jack Buzzard with Seattle chapter flag, 1997. *Photograph courtesy of Jack Buzzard.*

helped by embracing Santo Niño. There are good signs that their marriage is going to be all right. We have also started to bring a statue of Santo Niño into people's homes on invitation. Filipinos in Seattle from many different provinces in the Philippines have invited us, especially when they're being thankful. We read prayers while we're gathered in the family's house. Then we sing. We leave the statue and our prayer books there for a week and they pray every day. After a seven-day visit of the icon in the host's home, we take the statue home until another family wants it.

"We believe that if you have faith, all your prayers will be answered. When I pray to Santo Niño, I picture the whole thing from the Philippines—the big church where they light up the candles, people kneeling and moving towards the altar with a rosary." —MARCELA BUZZARD

9 KOREAN GOURD CUPS

Symbol of a Perfect Union

SONIA KIM

"It's only the first generation of Korean Americans, of my age or older, who would remember how cherished the gourd plants were. They had so many symbolic uses and stir so many childhood memories."—SONIA KIM

Growing up in a farming village

I grew up in the country, in a very small village in the Southern Choongnam Province of Korea. When I was growing up (before the Korean War), farming was the main way of life. Everybody knew everybody. People got together often. It was a very friendly, almost communal, way of life. New crops were shared, stories were shared,

Opposite:
Gourd cups. *Burke Museum collection. Photograph © 1999 Sam Van Fleet.*

Sonia Kim. *Photograph © 2000 Mary Randlett.*

Korean farmhouse with gourd vines, 1998. *Photograph courtesy of Sarah Loudon.*

mud walls capped with roofs thatched with rice stalks. The gourds grew up the roofs. When you planted the vine next to the fence, it crawled up over the fence and then went around and covered the roof of the fence or the house. First the vines grew and then white flowers bloomed. After that, fruit was formed. It took the gourds four to six months to mature. You had to let them dry on the vines until just before the frost came. The gourds needed to be mature inside and become hardened before you picked them. The vines made the farms beautiful. The fences were not really high, so we children could climb up on them in the summer nights, and look down from there. The gourd vines on the thatched roof were more beautiful than the ones growing in the garden.

When I think of the gourd, I remember the white petals when it was flowering. I didn't really notice them in daylight. But, in the night, when everything was quiet and the moon was out, the stars were shining, and the village people were resting, that was a very special time, and I noticed them then. Everybody would gather together in the courtyard and share food—steamed potatoes and corn, toasted green beans, fresh-picked wild mulberries—things you don't usually see in the cities. And we heard all the village stories: who was getting married, why they were doing it, whose child was having the one-hundredth-day celebration, where it was going to be, who was preparing food, who would put the tent up. While this was going on, the children would lie down on mats under the stars and the grandmothers would tell the stories. The white flowers of the gourds were part of that scene.

all the big special events were prepared together, and people helped each other. Everyone in the village helped each other and celebrated with each other. It was a good tradition that we lost. Life was peaceful, restful. Nothing was really hurried. There was no industrial noise. The sky was clear. It was a good childhood.

Almost everybody grew gourds. In farming villages, the houses were fenced around with

Story of Heungbu and Nolbu

The story of Heungbu and Nolbu is a morality tale, showing that good people get rewarded and bad people get punished. The gourd is part of the story. When you cut it open, there can be either treasure or filth inside, depending on your character. If you're good, you will find gold. If you're wicked and do things for a greedy purpose, then instead of gold, a monster may come out and punish you. I heard this story over and over in the courtyard at night. Even here in America, Korean children hear this story. Every-body knows the story. It's not just for children. It's a well-known morality tale.

Once upon a time, there lived two brothers on a Korean farm. Their names were Heungbu (the younger brother, whose name means "good," "prosperity") and Nolbu (the older brother, whose name means "lazy," "mean"). When their parents died, Nolbu got most of the rice paddies and became rich. Heungbu, who didn't get an inheritance, was poor.

One spring morning, Heungbu saw an injured swallow fall in front of his house. Heungbu, who was kind of heart, felt compassion toward the swallow and nursed it back to health. He then let it fly back to its own kind. In the spring, Heungbu saw the same swallow bring a small seed of a gourd. He planted the seed in his front garden with a happy heart. The gourd grew a large and beautiful fruit, which made the Heungbu family happy. When harvest time came, Heungbu sawed open the gourd and found that the inside was filled with gold. Heungbu became rich and happy.

Nolbu, who heard the story of Heungbu's sudden fortune, became jealous and wanted the same luck. But no swallow with a wounded leg came to Nolbu. So Nolbu captured a swallow and broke its leg. Then he nursed it back to health and sent it away. When the spring came, as expected, he saw a gourd seed brought by the swallow. Nolbu planted it, and it grew. But in the fall when he cut it open, instead of gold, the fruit had the filth of a monster, who punished the wicked older brother.

A perfect union and prosperity

The gourd is important in wedding ceremonies. It symbolizes the perfect union of yin and yang,

Korean gourd vine (*Lagenaria siceraria*). *Illustration by Arn Slettebak.*

❀ KOREAN WEDDINGS ❀

The traditional Korean wedding was a highly symbolic and carefully scripted ceremony. It grew out of Korea's rural past and reflected the heritage of its upper class. Usually the bride and groom did not meet until the ceremony itself. They wore elegant clothing and stood on mats in the courtyard of the bride's family home. Between them was a tall table piled high with special foods and symbolic objects.

Today, a wedding is more likely to take place in a public wedding hall, with the bride wearing white and the groom wearing a tuxedo. Whether traditional or contemporary, what has remained common to all Korean weddings is the *p'yebaek* (PEH-bek), the traditional greeting ceremony that follows the wedding. For this, the bride and groom put on Korean clothes and bow before the groom's parents. The bride serves wine and cooked meats to her new in-laws. They, in turn, bless the new couple and toss fruit into their laps, symbolizing their hope that the couple will "be fruitful and multiply."

Traditional Korean wedding. *Photograph courtesy of the Burke Museum.*

Contemporary Korean wedding. *Photograph courtesy of the Burke Museum.*

male and female, husband and wife. It is the confirmation of eternal bonding. The gourd is shaped like a heart—like a pear, eggplant, or pumpkin. To make gourd cups like those used in the wedding ceremony, you have to empty the inside. To accept a husband or wife, you have to empty yourself.

At the end of the traditional Korean wedding ceremony, the husband and wife drink wine from the gourd cups and then place them together, showing the consummation of the marriage, the uniting of themselves as one. The motion of putting the gourds together shows the symbolism of the perfect union. The pairing of gourd cups also symbolizes that half is incomplete. When the two halves unite, they make a perfect heart. That's how human beings are—interdependent. One without the other will not make it in this world.

After the wedding, the newly married couple bows to the bride's family and the groom's family. Just as in Genesis in the Bible, where God asks the people to be fruitful and multiply, Korean parents throw dates to the newly married couple and say, "Have many children." When gourds are opened, there are many seeds inside. This symbolizes the bearing of many children and the attainment of prosperity. For Koreans, family genealogy and the continuity of family traditions are very important; one way to show love for your parents is to give them lots of children.

After the gourd cups are used in the Korean wedding, the couple keeps them and uses them as decoration in their house. The cups aren't used as much today because there aren't as many traditional weddings, even in Korea. In more simplified, Western-style weddings where the only Korean part is greeting the families afterwards in a bowing ceremony, then regular wine glasses may be substituted for the gourd cups.

Have you scratched the *bagaji*?

Another use of the gourd is as a sound instrument to send a message between spouses. When a husband is neglecting his wife, or not doing the proper thing, the wife is supposed to "scratch the *bagaji* (bah-gah-jee)," or scratch the gourd. When we say, "Have you scratched the *bagaji*?" it means, "Have you been pointing things out to your husband?" It's an indirect way of showing that wives are not very content with what they're getting and there's some neglectful area the husband needs to correct. The scratching sound is kind of disturbing, so the husband will hear. Everybody knows the meaning of "*bagaji*" and understands the humor.

Different meanings associated with different uses

Gourds grow to different sizes. Some mature to the small wedding-cup size. Others become much larger. Depending on their size, we use them for different things. If they're big, we use them to store rice, wash rice, or carry rice wine. When birds try to eat the rice, we rattle a smaller gourd, and the sound makes the birds go away. If the gourd is small, we use it as a dipper.

With the different uses also come other symbolic meanings. Shamans, for example, use a gourd in healing and other ceremonies. When a gourd is dry on the inside, it rattles when shaken.

Humorous painted gourds of groom and bride. *Photograph courtesy of Kay Hong.*

If you shake it, the noise discourages bad ghosts and chases bad spirits away. When somebody is ill, shamans put the gourd dipper on the wooden floor, upside down, and then scratch the floor with the gourd. It produces a sound that makes the cause of the illness go away. The person will then be healed.

The gourd is also good for sanitary purposes, because it doesn't get dirty inside. If you dip water and then put the gourd upside down, it dries fast and it's clean. You can find gourd dippers at mineral springs, often found on the way to the temples on the high mountains. There are special medicinal springs up there that are purified by the mountains, especially in the early morning before the dewdrops come. A half gourd is there for people to dip into the water and take a drink and be healed.

A mystery of life

I have not seen gourd vines growing here in America, but a friend of mine showed me a painted gourd with a bride's face. She said it was given to her as a wedding gift. The bride's face was made up with red blush circles on both cheeks and humorously protruded lips painted in rosy pink, reaching out to kiss her groom!

The expressive face on that gourd brought back a host of memories of my childhood in Korea. Instantly, I was transported back to my hometown of fifty years ago. I saw a vivid picture of myself entranced with the gourd flowers on the thatched roof of my old country house. In

Respect for family—the Confucian ideal of filial piety—is a central focus of Korean life. The father is the head of the household, and family membership is defined through the male line. When a woman marries, she becomes part of her husband's family. The family tree, or *chokpo* (JOK-poh), records a family's lineage and can trace family membership back hundreds of years. Because continuity of this record can be maintained only through the male line, Koreans have placed a premium on having sons. Although much has changed in modern Korea, one's social position as documented in the *chokpo* is a treasured possession, carefully handed down from one generation to the next.

daylight they usually seemed plain and barely noticeable, but when the summer moon shone upon the white petals of the gourd flowers while the whole village was asleep at night, they seemed to exude a mysterious beauty of a rare, almost heavenly, quality. My heart was enveloped in the stillness of the night. It was then I discovered a different way of looking at nature. In that moment of silence, I felt that I was merging and becoming one with the flowers. That precious feeling left a long-lasting imprint on my young psyche.

Since we began talking about the symbolic meanings of the gourd and the stories of Heungbu and Nolbu, I have been contemplating deeply buried memories of my childhood and the mystery of life. It has made me want to get back to the much-cherished old customs of sharing with and caring for our neighbors. It may not be possible to re-create the magic of my childhood, but I wonder why it is so difficult to create the magical bonding of two hearts, "the emptying of yourself" to make room for another human being?

10 JAPANESE *OBUTSUDAN*

Altar to Remember Loved Ones

REVEREND DEAN KOYAMA

"Being a Buddhist minister, I have to say that the most meaningful object for me is the obutsudan. *It's the Buddhist family altar that is in almost every Japanese household. It's usually handed down to the oldest son of a family, so it has been the center of a household for years. The* obutsudan *at my house belonged to my wife's grandparents, who brought it here from Japan."*

—REVEREND DEAN KOYAMA

Opposite:

Obutsudan. *Burke Museum collection. Photograph © 1999 Sam Van Fleet.*

Reverend Dean Koyama. *Photograph © 2000 Mary Randlett.*

Taking refuge in Amida Buddha

There are three main objects of reverence that can be placed in a Jodo Shinshu *obutsudan* (oh-BOOT-zoo-dahn): a statue of Amida Buddha, a picture of Amida Buddha, or the Chinese characters "Namo Amida Butsu" (NAH-moh ah-MEE-dah BOOT-zoo), which mean "I take refuge in Amida Buddha." Amida Buddha represents the ultimate in wisdom and compassion, which are the two elements that compose enlightenment. Rennyo, a Japanese Buddhist leader in the fifteenth century, made the *obutsudan* style with the characters very popular because, he said, "Better than a wooden statue is to have a picture of Amida Buddha, and better than a picture of Amida Buddha, is to have the characters 'Namo Amida Butsu.'" The saying "Namo Amida Butsu" is the core of a Jodo Shinshu Buddhist's life, and it's easier to keep the phrase in our hearts than to keep a physical object or a picture.

On the *obutsudan*, usually in the front, should be offerings of flowers, incense, and a candle. The flowers represent the ephemeral nature of this world. The incense symbolically links the material and spiritual worlds. The candle represents wisdom. There are food offerings as well.

A place to focus and remember our loved ones

To me, the *obutsudan* is really just a center, a place where we can focus upon things other than Nintendo and other worldly goods. It's a place where we can focus and remember our loved ones, and try to be mindful of the wisdom and compassion in our lives. Whether it's a big *obutsudan* or a little one, the important thing is that we have a space and a place as a reminder.

Usually, the first thing we do in the morning is make an offering. Nowadays it can be of anything, but traditionally it was of rice, because that was the first food cooked for the day. Rice would be offered to the altar, incense would be burned, and then the people making the offering would have a service and chant a sutra, the recorded words of the Buddha. Typically, that's how the day would start. I remember how, after my mom passed away, my father would bring an offering of a cup of coffee in front of the *obutsudan* because my mother liked to drink coffee in the morning. It's a connection to, and a reminder of, the important people in our lives. We have a physical spot to have that connection to the people who have passed away, our loved ones.

It doesn't have to be a very organized activity. It just happens when it happens. Usually my dad would make the offering first thing in the morning. He left to go to work very early, and so we probably weren't even awake yet when it happened. In my family, now, we have young boys, so we try to gather them together in front of the *obutsudan* at least once a day. It's hard, because the kids wake up at different times. Sometimes when the two older ones are off to school, the youngest one is just waking up. So we try to do it right before dinner. We gather in front of the *obutsudan* and burn incense and try to be mindful of the Buddha.

Back in Japan, and even in the United States soon after the immigration of Japanese people, extended families lived as one household.

Many Japanese families have Buddhist altars, or *obutsudan*, in their homes, which are decorated with food and flowers in honor of their deceased loved ones. A family member opens the altar each morning and makes an offering of the first food cooked that day—usually rice—and closes the altar at night. In the center of the cabinet is a statue of the Amida Buddha, the Buddha of infinite wisdom and compassion. The gesture of the right hand represents light and wisdom; the outstretched left hand represents compassion. Furnishings of the altar may include a book containing the death dates of ancestors and hanging model lanterns, the light of which symbolizes the ancestors' wisdom. There are also offerings of food, flowers, and incense.

Reverend Koyama and his family at the *obutsudan* in their home. *Photograph © 1999 Sam Van Fleet.*

Usually the children would see the grandparents going in front of the *obutsudan* and conducting the services. That's how children learned about the different customs of Buddhism—from the grandparents. But now everyone lives in separate homes and traditions are getting lost. Parents are too busy to take part in these customs. It really takes a great effort on the part of parents today to try and continue with these different kinds of traditions.

That's one of the things I'm trying to encourage at our temple, to get people to at least go to the *obutsudan* once a day. I try and talk about the customs and ask the kids whether they go to the *obutsudan*.

There are many ways we use the *obutsudan*. We sometimes visit my wife's mother in Sacramento. Usually, when we arrive, the first thing we do is go in front of the *obutsudan* at her house and burn incense to mark my wife's history for the kids. Then, when we're ready to go back to Seattle, we do the same thing. That's how an *obutsudan* can be used as well.

One day, after playing baseball with my kids, some friends went out and bought cookies and candy for my kids, to thank them for playing baseball with them. Then the kids, right away, took cookies and candies and put them in front of the altar as an offering of appreciation. Each one put a cookie or a piece of candy on top to show respect for the items they had received.

Sizes and styles may change, but the meaning remains

Typically, an *obutsudan* is hand-crafted out of wood. It's painted with black lacquer and a lot of gold leaf. They tend to be very expensive nowadays. The *obutsudan* at the Burke Museum is a beautiful example of one that would be found in a household in Japan but, because of its large size, not in a household in the United States. In Japan, families would have a special room with a designated corner alcove from floor to ceiling for the family altar. Here in the United States, when you go to the home of a Buddhist family, the *obutsudan* might be smaller—about two to three feet tall—so it can be put on top of a table.

Family homes here, nowadays, are getting very cluttered. To have a big *obutsudan* takes up a lot of space. People usually would rather have a very simple one in their home. But it would still have the same meaning. I think a lot of the change in the *obutsudan* probably has to do with space. Typically, in Japan, when the oldest son inherits the *obutsudan,* he also inherits the house. When his family moves into the house, the *obutsudan* is there as well. But in the United States, to try and move an *obutsudan* that size can be very cumbersome. And here, furniture changes so easily and people seem to move quite often. To have a permanent *obutsudan* may not be best. But to have at least a reminder of one is a good idea.

These days people are making *obutsudan* that aren't very traditional but are abbreviated or modified versions. Some members of my temple made small *obutsudan* onto which we can affix a scroll and use it that way. Some are made in plastic or acrylic with a picture or scroll. I use a small one when I go to cemeteries and do a graveside service. We set up a small *obutsudan* and burn incense. No matter what its shape or size is, or what it looks like, the strength of the meaning is still the same.

Obon combines the religious and the festive

There isn't that much difference between private observance at home, when families go in front of the *obutsudan* on a daily basis, and public observance at Obon (oh-BOHN) each summer. I always think about how Obon is traditionally observed in Japan. Often people move away

Obutsudan altars, tabletop style. *Photographs © 1999 Sam Van Fleet.*

Obon celebration, Seattle, 1998. *Photograph by Miriam Kahn.*

Jenny Nakahara Eng, Obon, Seattle, 1998. *Photograph by Miriam Kahn.*

❀ OBON ❀

Obon, the most important summertime festival in Japan, is celebrated in the middle of the seventh lunar month when the moon is full. During Obon, people honor and express their gratitude to their ancestors. It is especially important for those who have lost a loved one in the preceding year. Although devoted to the dead, Obon is a happy event, celebrated with much feasting and dancing. Many Obon customs are to welcome the spirits, feed and entertain them, and then bid them farewell again. Spirits of the dead visit their descendants in the world of the living, attracted by the strength of familial ties, food offerings on family altars, and light. Obon is also known as the Lantern Festival because painted lanterns and small fires are lit under the moonlight to help guide the spirits.

Most Japanese apply the practice of different religions (Buddhism, Shintoism, and now Christianity) to different stages of human life. Death is the province of Buddhism, and Obon is a Buddhist festival. Obon has been celebrated in Japan since the seventh century and was originally held only at the imperial court. As Buddhism spread throughout Japan and became popular with the common people, the festival spread with it, changing in character from a solemn religious service to a lively and joyous event. In the past, the service honoring the ancestors was conducted privately in the home. Today, Japanese Americans also celebrate in public at Buddhist temples.

Dances called Bon Odori (bohn oh-doh-ree) are performed at the Obon festival to honor the contributions ancestors have made to the dancers' lives. Men and women of all ages form a line, which develops into a spiral, as if moving up toward the moon. Some dances are of remembrance and gratitude. Others represent traditional activities like fishing or mining. Depending on the song, dancers carry appropriate items such as fans, umbrellas, baskets, or bells. Bon Odori dances were brought to the United States by the first Japanese immigrants and are now popular in many Japanese American communities. *Taiko* drumming accompanies the dancing.

Bon Odori dancers with fans, Seattle, 1998. *Photograph by Miriam Kahn.*

from their parents' homes in the countryside or small villages and go to jobs in the cities and live in apartments. But during Obon season they make the trip back home to their parents. While everyone is gathered together at Obon, they conduct a service. Obon sparks that tradition of calling back all the family to come home. You have everyone in one place and, in that way, it's easy to remember your deceased loved ones, your ancestors. Here in the United States, families are also scattered, but Obon doesn't have as big an impact in pulling everyone together as it does in Japan. You don't call up your cousin and say, "You know, it's Obon time. Are you coming home for the summer?" The answer would be, "No, I'm going to Disneyland for vacation instead."

Combining activities at the *obutsudan* with *taiko* (TYE-koh) drumming (see next chapter) gets to the whole nature of what Obon represents. It's basically two-sided. One side is religious and the other is festive. That's where the *taiko* drum comes in. During the festival dancing there's usually a big *taiko* drum that someone is hitting to help keep the beat of the music and help keep the dancers in step. By the very nature of Obon, there isn't a conflict between the *obutsudan* and the *taiko*, the religious and the festive aspects. The private aspect of one's religious life, and the sharing of that life in public, culminates with the festival, with the drumming.

Reverend Kumata's *obutsudan*

The *obutsudan* at the Burke Museum belonged to Reverend Kumata, who was the head minister of the Seattle *betsuin* (head temple of the district). He brought the *obutsudan* over from Japan. It was in his home for a while, and then his family donated it to the Seattle *betsuin*. When it was loaned to the Burke Museum, it

Bon Odori dancers with fans, Seattle, 1998. *Photograph by Miriam Kahn.*

was no longer being used in the temple as an altar but was downstairs in storage.

Reverend Kumata was the first Nisei (NEE-say)—that's a second-generation Japanese born in the United States—to become a head minister of the Seattle *betsuin*. Being an English-speaking American citizen during the war, he had the formidable task of trying to keep the peace between the Buddhist temples and the United States government. During that time, one of the first things the government did was to take over the temples and put the ministers in internment camps. Reverend Kumata had to act as the interpreter for the interrogations. After the war, when people were released from the camps, he went up and down the West Coast trying to help open up the temples again.

We recently observed the one hundredth anniversary of our Buddhist organization on the mainland of the United States.

11 JAPANESE *TAIKO*

Drum for Learning about Culture

SEATTLE MATSURI TAIKO

Opposite:

Taiko drum. *Ethnomusicology collection, School of Music, University of Washington. Photograph © 2001 Sam Van Fleet.*

Seattle Matsuri Taiko (from left to right: Justin Cross, Carole Furuya, Donna Zumoto, Jenny Nakahara Eng, Leslie Fisher, Nicole Shimizu). *Photograph © 2000 Mary Randlett.*

"I think taiko *gives you a sense of connection to your heritage. My brother joined Seattle Matsuri Taiko early on, so when I was really young I was always at practice and at all the performances. I always remember* taiko. *And* taiko *has always been a part of Bon Odori, part of the church. It also brings up interest in different cultural things."* —NICOLE SHIMIZU

From practical beginnings to a new performing art

When you read about ancient cultures, you read a lot about music. The drum is something that started very early. It's simple to play. Drumming has always been a centerpiece of ancient music, and *taiko* (TYE-koh) is the same way—it just developed in Asia instead of North America or Europe.

Taiko began more than a thousand years ago as a practical instrument—a drum. It used to be all about the community, part of the life of Japanese farming villages. Drumming could be used for things like calling people to clear the fields, gathering people together for an event, celebrating Shinto religious festivals, or creating sound effects for Kabuki (kah-BOO-key) theater.

Later, especially since World War II, *taiko* became more of a form of entertainment. As time went by, in about the early 1970s, Seichi Tanaka, who was trained in Japan, brought *taiko* to San Francisco. He was the first person to

bring it over from Japan and start teaching it in the United States. Now it's more like any type of music that you listen to and watch, a performing art. *Taiko* is used more for festivals today. Because its original purpose was for communication through villages, *taiko* had to be really loud. But as it became a performing art, it combined both the loud sound and the skillful way of playing it very softly.

Taiko isn't as easy as it looks. When you observe someone playing, it looks easy. But there are so many different styles. That's the difficult thing. Each group has its unique style. Our group struggles with finding our own style. The visual part of *taiko* is just as important as the sound. You can't really separate the two. When you talk about *taiko* style, it includes everything from moving around physically to moving your arms to moving your sticks—even to the way you place the drum stands and the way you stand when you play the drum. In *taiko*, pretty much everything becomes part of your style.

Most of the songs are celebratory. Some are very old. Many are written by artists to give an emotion to a place, like one song called "Hachijo," which is a classic. Hachijo is the name

Chris Visaya, Tsunami Taiko. *Photographs © Chana Meddin.*

of an island off the coast of Japan. The main rhythm of the song was written by an ancient warrior who was exiled to Hachijo as a prisoner of war. The songs we play are basically songs we hear and like. There's a certain repertoire, but we do our own version. We've been trying to make up our own. It takes a lot of time and effort.

A good way to learn about our culture

"The first time I learned how to play *taiko* was in high school. It was for a cultural assembly in which each of the student groups from different ethnic backgrounds had to participate. A group of friends and I tried to think of something that would reflect Japanese cul-

ture. We'd just seen a *taiko* group from Los Angeles perform at the Seattle Obon [oh-BOHN] festival and thought it was kind of interesting. My Sunday school teacher at church had just formed the first *taiko* group in Seattle. We asked him if he could teach us how to play, to learn something about our Japanese culture. We learned a few songs for the assembly, borrowed some drums, showed up at school, got into *happi* [HAH-pee] coats [festival coats], and went up on stage. It was a lot of fun. A few years later, we were looking for something to do, something with the church. We thought back on our first experience with *taiko* and decided to pursue that, and that eventually led to the formation of Seattle Matsuri Taiko. We thought *taiko* would be a good way to learn about

❀ *TAIKO* DRUMMING ❀

Taiko drums, following the paths of Buddhism, first arrived in Japan from China and Korea in the fifth century. They continue to be used in traditional Japanese court music, which has changed little over the centuries. In addition, Japanese regional folk styles of *taiko* have developed that are tied to festivals and religious rites. But the type of group drum-

ming that is popular today, in which several performers play drums of various sizes, with some keeping the beat and others playing a solo, arose in Japan after World War II. During the counterculture movement of the late 1960s, Japanese youth turned to folk arts that had been neglected during the rapid modernization and Western bias of the postwar

era. In the United States, Japanese American youth began to explore *taiko* during the same turbulent times, trying to define themselves in opposition to the rigid assimilationist outlook of their parents' generation and the American stereotype of the "quiet Japanese.""

❀ THE TWO SIDES OF OBON ❀

The totality of Obon is represented by the combination of its private and public aspects: the contemplative making of an offering at the family *obutsudan* and the booming *taiko* drumming at the festival. As Dean Koyama said, Obon is two-sided, one being religious and private, and the other festive and public. Both aspects serve the purpose of allowing people to pay respect to their loved ones. Both family *obutsudan* and *taiko* performances help Japanese Americans to learn about, maintain, and share their culture. Reverend Koyama's son, Toshi, embodies this desire for the young to learn the ways of their parents and grandparents. In the first photo, taken at age three (1994), Toshi intently watches *taiko* drummers perform at Seattle's Obon celebration, tapping along with them on his own small drum. In the second photo, taken at age seven (1998), he is making an offering to his grandfather at his family's *obutsudan* while his family looks on.

Toshi Koyama playing a drum during Obon, Seattle.
Photograph © 1994 Chana Meddin.

our culture and to meet other people. Speaking for myself, I wasn't too aware of many aspects of my Japanese culture. I was pretty much completely Americanized. I don't speak any Japanese. We learned more about *taiko* over the years, especially from visiting groups. We learned all about the origins of *taiko*, how it was brought over to the United States, and how it has developed into an art form. We got to know professional Japanese drummers and learned a lot from them."—ROBERT HAMATANI

"As parents, we were happy because *taiko* gave the kids the interest in their heritage and it made them want to learn more about Japan. They approached us and said, 'We'd like to go to Japan.' So we backed them. For 50 percent of the kids it was their first or second time to go there."—JOYCE SHIMIZU

"My interest in *taiko* started at Nichiren Buddhist Church. The reverend was offering some classes in *taiko*, tea ceremony, and Japanese dancing, but then had to leave to go back to Japan. Soon thereafter, Seattle Matsuri Taiko had an open session where you

Toshi Koyama at family *obutsudan*. *Photograph © 1998 Sam Van Fleet.*

could come and watch them perform. I came to that with a friend and was interested. That got me back into *taiko*. I was always interested in Japanese culture. Both my mom and dad are from Japan. At home, my mom speaks Japanese and my dad speaks English."
—JENNY NAKAHARA ENG

"*Taiko's* still fun even though I've been doing it for nine years now. I've learned a lot. I've learned more about my culture and Japanese traditional values. I also like the camaraderie between everybody in the group. We get along pretty well. On long trips we always have fun. But *taiko* to me is learning about the culture, the past and the future, and showing it to other people."—BEN DODOBARA

"*Taiko* is an important part of our lives. We make a great sacrifice for it. During the summer we have a very rigorous performance schedule. We practice at least once a week. Obviously I like playing. I like these people. That's probably one of the biggest reasons that I stay in the group. But I think one of the reasons I joined is that it's such a nonmainstream activity, yet it has the attraction of promoting our cultural heritage. Within the melting pot of the United States, how do you hold on to your heritage? How do you hold on to who you are? This is the main reason, I think, why we play *taiko*. The performing part is secondary. When we perform, a lot of people can see how we express ourselves, but the accolades that come from performing are less important than learning about our heritage."—CLIFFORD OZAKI

Seattle Matsuri Taiko

We started out kind of loosely as a youth group in 1986 and 1987. Somewhere around then we

Making noodles for Obon, Seattle (left, Yasuko Nakahara, and right, Etsuko Shimbo). *Photograph © 1994 Chana Meddin.*

officially became Matsuri Taiko, meaning "festival *taiko*." Our group grew to nine people. Just about every weekend in the spring or summer, you'll find *taiko* being played. Every weekend in July, we play somewhere. Because of our affiliation with the church—we're the only group in Seattle sponsored by a church—we perform at the local Obon festivals.

A lot of our ties are to the church. The church lets us use their gym every Thursday night to practice, and their space all year round to store our drums. In exchange, we clean the gym every month and set it up for different functions. At Obon we make *somen* (SOH-men) (cold noodles) and at the bazaar we make *udon* (oo-don) (hot noodles) to make money for the church. When someone wants to join our group, one of the first things we ask is if they have a problem with having to do all these things for the church.

✸ *TAIKO* DRUMS ✸

In Japan, most *taiko* drums are made by hollowing out a tree trunk and then stretching an animal skin over the opening. Kinnara Taiko, the first *taiko* group to spring directly from the Japanese American community (in Los Angeles), came up with a clever and much more economical innovation for making drums outside Japan. They used oak wine barrels, without which *taiko* probably would never have developed the way it did in North America. Kinnara Taiko devised a way to stretch the skin using car jacks, which has now become a standard method.

Making a *taiko* drum from a wine barrel.
Photograph © 1994 Chana Meddin.

Some of the other groups focus on *taiko* only. They rent a space to practice and a space to store their drums. If we had to rent space, it would cost us quite a bit of money. We are very fortunate. When we perform somewhere, we usually ask for a donation, and then use the money to maintain our equipment, to sponsor guest instructors, and to cover travel expenses.

We make the drums ourselves. We buy wine barrels and take them apart and sand the strips individually and glue them back together. To finish them, we put fiberglass on the inside to give them strength. We were taught how to stretch the cowhide over the end of the drum using tire jacks. Then we tack the skin down with decorative *taiko* nails. We made a bunch of

Masaye
Nakagawa
adding nails.
*Photograph
© 1994
Chana Meddin.*

Above:
Junzo Nakagawa making a drum.
Photograph © 1994 Chana Meddin.

Right:
Masaye Nakagawa making a drum using a car jack.
Photograph © 1994 Chana Meddin.

drums when we were first starting out. There's a *taiko* Web site we use that lists suppliers all across the country. In Tokyo, there's a wonderful store we go to. For the very small drum, the *shimedaiko* (SHEE-meh-DYE-koh), each skin was at least three or four hundred dollars, and you need two skins. And for the bigger drum, the *odaiko* (o-DYE-koh), each skin was thousands of dollars. They're all on our wish list, but we can't afford them right now.

People know us as the people in the purple costumes. It's interesting, because some of the other *taiko* groups have two or three costumes and vary them, but we predominantly wear purple. We like our purple. And purple is sort of the church color, too.

Seattle Matsuri Taiko, Nicole Shimizu (center), Seattle, 1998.
Photograph by Miriam Kahn.

Seattle Matsuri Taiko, Seattle, 1998. *Photograph by Miriam Kahn.*

Performing is secondary, but fun

The funnest part is performing, showing every-one else the Japanese culture of *taiko*. Because we do so many of the festivals in the summer,

we play for a wide variety of people. It surprises us all the time that we'll play these songs over and over in practice and then when we perform— like when we played at the opening for the new REI building downtown—everyone gets quiet and gathers and watches.

It's good exercise, too. After half an hour of performance, you feel pretty drained, especially in the summer. Recently we had two perfor-mances down in Oregon, with only three or four hours in between. One was at the opening of an Uwajimaya store in Beaverton. Driving back that night, we wondered whether we were going to make it home.

Each time before we perform, we give a brief background about *taiko*. Most people think, "Oh gee, Japanese people are quiet and everyone is very studious." People always identify Asians with engineering and science and that type of field. It's unusual for people to see *taiko*, because it's so loud, with people yelling and screaming. These people, next to whom audience members might work, and who are very reserved at work, are running around carrying big sticks. It's kind of important to give them some background about what *taiko* is all about.

After we play, people show lots of apprecia-tion. They say, "Wow, I was really surprised," and "Whoa, I've never seen this before. That was cool." It makes us feel good. They ask us if we practice four times a week. It's funny when they ask if we have physical training, some kind of regimen. Yeah, some of us walk the dog in the morning! We walk from our cars into the building! We get asked a lot if we're from here. People are kind of surprised that we're all from Seattle.

❀ *TAIKO* AS A LIVING ART FORM ❀

The particular type of *taiko* that developed in North America—and there are over one hundred groups on the continent, most of which were formed in the '80s and '90s—has only tenuous roots in Japan. No Buddhist group in Japan plays *taiko* the same way that *taiko* groups in North America play. *Taiko* that has developed here is a uniquely American form. The development of *taiko* in North America is a flexible adaptation of original traditions to fit new surroundings. This is what makes *taiko* a truly living and evolving art form. As Ben Dodobara said, *"taiko* is learning about the culture, the past, *and* the future."

Left:
Glen Shimbo, Obon, Seattle. *Photograph © 1994 Chana Meddin.*

Above:
Howard Nakanishi, Seattle. *Photograph © 1994 Chana Meddin.*

Seattle Matsuri Taiko, Seattle, 1998. *Photograph by Miriam Kahn.*

12 CHINESE NEW YEAR FOODS

Meals that Bring Families Together

MAXINE CHAN, with RON CHEW, DONNIE CHIN, HELEN KAY, and LAURA WONG-WHITEBEAR

"Chinese celebrations all revolve around eating and fellowship. Food is a very important part of family life. Some foods have special significance during different celebrations."—HELEN KAY

Everything revolves around food

In China, everything revolves around food, from the very beginning when you meet someone. In the United States, the normal greeting is "How are you?" In China, it's "Have you eaten yet? Have you had your rice yet?" We don't ask how your grandmother is. It's about the food.

Through food you learn a lot about people's cultures. If you start examining why food is

Opposite:
Chinese New Year food display. *Burke Museum collection. Photograph © 1999 Sam Van Fleet.*

Maxine Chan. *Photograph © 1999 Mary Randlett.*

Chinese Characters for New Year. *Characters drawn by Min-chih Chou.*

important, what kind of food we eat, how we eat, how we prepare it, how we serve it, when we serve it, and the symbolism, it's all about culture, it's not just food. China is so vast, and the resources available were very limited—like land to grow wheat, grain, or rice. There wasn't a lot of land to grow enough wheat to feed lots of animals, so there was less use of meat. How we cook food—stir-frying—is about conserving resources. Also, in China there were famines, and that may be why food played an important part in people's lives. It's a scarce commodity for a lot of people.

There's a lot of symbolism in the type of food that is picked for holidays like New Year. Each of the dishes represents something. The New Year holiday is celebrated by all the generations, from way back then to today, and using almost the same types of foods. It hasn't changed that much. One of the traditions is that you open New Year with a dinner at midnight in which you take two helpings of everything to show that you're prosperous and will have good fortune for

the coming year. It's important to be able to take two helpings, even if they're very small, to show you can afford to have two.

"I come from a bicultural background. My mother was Native American and my father was Chinese. My father never really taught us a lot of traditional things, but one thing that we always did, and that I knew was important, was the Chinese New Year and having the dinner. We lived in Tacoma and would come to Seattle every year to celebrate. I grew up knowing that this was the one thing that Chinese people did and that this was part of my heritage. But my father never really explained. I think it was later on that I became curious about it and learned that there is something special about the number of courses and about what foods are served."—LAURA WONG-WHITEBEAR

Picking a good menu

It's very important to know how to pick a good menu. You're revered if you know how. Picking a good menu means getting all the right ingredients together—having the fish, the chicken, and the noodles—because of all the symbolism. If you go to a restaurant, you have to be able to

❀ EVERY FOOD HAS MEANING ❀

Dishes vary according to family and region, but often include certain mainstays because of their symbolic meaning. The vegetarian dish "Buddhist feast of the monks," which always has an odd number of ingredients, reminds people to be humble and to care for all living things. A whole chicken represents the phoenix rising out of the ashes, or rebirth. The fatty chicken tail is given to the eldest person, a custom indicating respect that originated in times when food was often scarce. A whole fish symbolizes abundance. Long noodles indicate long life.

understand the strength of that restaurant.

The *fat choy* (faht choy), or hair seaweed, and the *ho see* (hoh see), or dried oysters—those are puns. *Fat* means to be prosperous and good. *Ho see* means good business. That's why people serve certain foods, because there's a pun that gives it meaning.

Things vary from family to family. Depending upon the family, you might serve different things. Beyond the main foods, some people have *hoi tom* (hoy tom), or sea cucumber soup. Some have a lot of New Year's pastries. Some don't have any. Certain people know how to cook certain things better than other people. It isn't precise.

Fong Lee Yee O making New Year cake, Seattle.
Photographs © 2001 Natalie B. Fobes.

Chinese New Year, a time of ritual cleansing and renewal, is one of the most important annual occasions in the Chinese calendar. Although details of how it is celebrated vary from family to family and region to region, the customs associated with Chinese New Year have roots that go back more than 2,000 years. These customs carry symbolic meanings about fertility, wholeness, family, fortune, and health. The new year is celebrated on the second new moon after the winter solstice. During the time preceding it, families prepare by cleaning their houses, settling their debts, shopping for gifts, and preparing special foods. As the day draws near, they visit their friends and relatives and exchange gifts. Eating the New Year's meal together is traditionally a time of family togetherness.

Preparing New Year's dinner, Seattle (from left to right: Helen Kay, Anne Ko, Joyce Yip). *Photograph © 1998 Sam Van Fleet.*

Scallions and greens. *Photograph © 1998 Sam Van Fleet.*

"Usually we have a chicken with the head."
—MAXINE CHAN

"As a Chinese American, my mom always made fried chicken. And we ate monk's food. My dad lived with monks, so we ate lots of pickled food and soybean, and mock duck made from soybean."
—DONNIE CHIN

"We always had the *sai foon* [sye foon], or bean threads. That was standard, partly because my mom liked to make it."—RON CHEW

A time for family to gather

Chinese New Year is an important time for the family to get together. Oftentimes, people are out doing their thing. The new year symbolically gives you a chance to get together and talk to relatives you typically don't see because everyone is working and busy. Usually the New Year's meal is a very boisterous event, with lots of talking and food dripping from people's mouths. You try not to dwell too much on bad things. It's not considered good.

"In my family, when I was a little kid, they would wake me up at midnight. I'd ask, 'Can I eat my two

☸ WHY DOES THE LION DANCE? ☸

The lion dances to chase away evil spirits and bring good luck. Today, lion dancers go from business to business "eating" lettuce and red envelopes of money. The Chinese word for "lettuce" sounds like the word for "good fortune."

Lion dance, King Street, Seattle, 1921. *Wing Luke Asian Museum, Willard Jue Collection.*

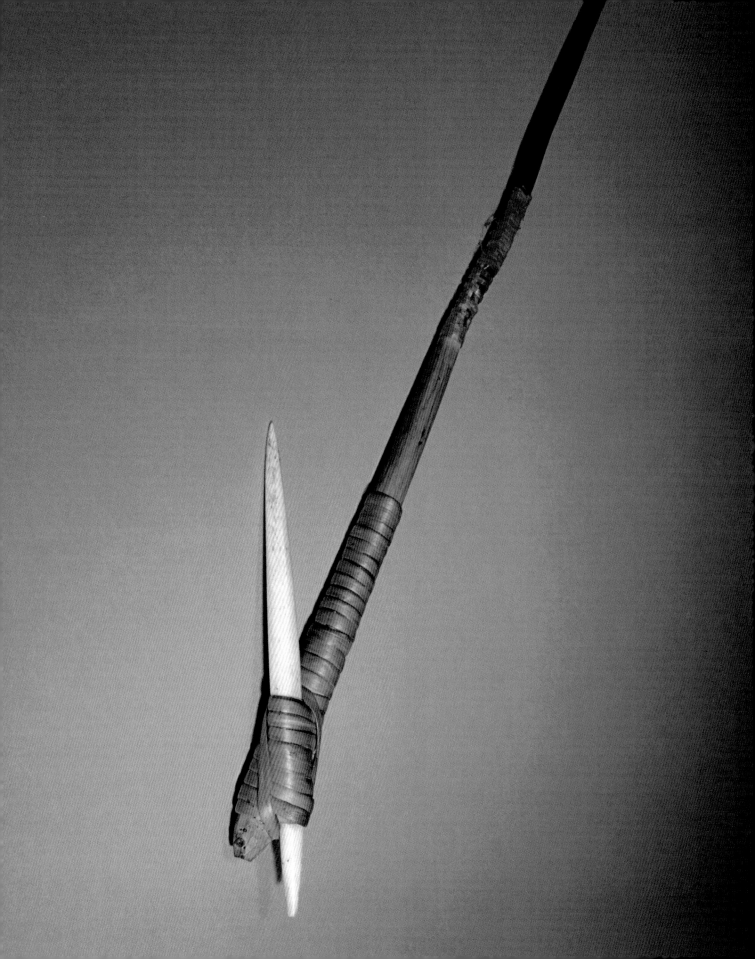

13 COAST SALISH FISH HOOK

Reminder of the Importance of Salmon

LEONARD FORSMAN

"I remember being at West Point, an archaeological site next to Seattle's Discovery Park, and finding one of those little bone points, which is the only thing that survives in an archaeological site. The cedar bark rots away over time, as does the wood that it's mounted on. All you have left of the hook is this one little reminder of all that's involved in catching salmon."—LEONARD FORSMAN

Fish hooks

Fish hooks bring to mind the importance of salmon fishing within our Suquamish (soo-ꜰꜱʜ-mish) culture and the importance of the fisher people who are involved in harvesting

Opposite:
Salmon fish hook. *Burke Museum collection. Photograph © 1999 Sam Van Fleet.*

Leonard Forsman. *Photograph © 2000 Mary Randlett.*

❀ FIRST SALMON CEREMONY ❀

The First Salmon Ceremony acknowledges the profound and enduring relationship between Native people and salmon. It prescribes a moral code of behavior that includes instruction about taking care of the earth's resources. To this day, the first salmon caught in the spring is honored in religious ceremonies that, although they vary from tribe to tribe, include prayers, cooking, presentation of the salmon, and returning the salmon's bones to the water.

salmon. When I think about that fish hook, I think about the first person who made one, who that person was, and how they came up with this idea. I think about how they put the different parts together and about when it worked the first time. It was a long, long time ago, and that person could have had a certain amount of power. Maybe that person was a mythical or a

supernatural being, as we call them now. The farther back we go, the less defined the boundary is between the "real" world and the spirit world.

That fish hook and the intricate way cedar was used to hold it together is something for us to remember—that it took a lot of work to get that salmon into your canoe. Not only did you have to create the perfect hook, but you had to have the bait, the weight, and the place to fish for the salmon. You had to have your canoe together, you had to know when the fish were

First Salmon Ceremony: carrying the salmon to the longhouse.
Photograph © 1991 Natalie B. Fobes.

First Salmon Ceremony: returning the salmon's bones to the water. *Photograph © 1991 Natalie B. Fobes*

there, and you had to know when they were biting. You also needed to be a person who was prepared in a ceremonial way and was worthy of catching those salmon—of having the Salmon People come to your hook and choose to be caught.

Bringing back the First Salmon Ceremony

The First Salmon Ceremony represents the spiritual connection between the Native people of Puget Sound and the salmon they depend on for food. The Salmon People live deep under the sea and are Indian people like us. Every year they choose to transform themselves into salmon and return to our waters to provide food for our ceremonies and our daily lives. The first salmon that comes back is the leader. We thank the leader in a ceremonial way, so that he and his people will know we are thankful. If they believe we are grateful and respectful, they keep returning every year. By not wasting fish, by keeping

the rivers and creeks clean and honoring their return in a ceremony, the salmon will keep us culturally and physically alive.

I don't know when the last First Salmon Ceremony was for the Suquamish. We don't have a river, so we didn't have a place to wait for the first salmon to show up. If we did go to a river, it was in somebody else's territory, where we had an agreement with them to be there, were related to someone from there, or had established rights to fish there. Some anthropologists have likened Agate Pass to the "Suquamish River." One elder recalls that there was a tradition of catching the first salmon of the season there, at the mouth of the passage.

Recently, there has been talk about bringing the First Salmon Ceremony back to the Suquamish. If this happens, it's going to be a very important cultural event.

Salmon have long been an important resource for the Native people of the Northwest Coast—not only for food but for cultural sustenance as well. From ancient times, salmon have been caught in a variety of ways, using hooks, spears, nets, weirs, and traps. As pioneering settlers moved into the Northwest, they brought with them different fishing technologies and a commercial orientation to fishing that eventually took its toll on the health and abundance of the salmon runs. Conflicts also arose over access to good fishing spots, in spite of the fact that treaties between the tribes and the U.S. government had granted Native people the "right of taking fish at all usual and accustomed places." Prior to the arrival of outsiders, access to local fishing spots was regulated by inheritance, marriage, or political agreement.

Remembering what's important

We continue to understand our important role with the salmon in a spiritual and cultural way—being responsible for putting salmon back into the system because of their importance to us. Environmentally, we continue to push to try to protect the watershed and other things, to protect the salmon. The tribe puts a lot of resources into salmon enhancement. But we also think of salmon as less of an industry or occupation than we used to. We've kind of forgotten about its importance to us economically.

I remember the times I went fishing out in Agate Pass with my father and how important it was for him to be able to harvest fish again with his sons. The importance of this activity to our young people is great. It not only brings families together but also brings the tribe together as a whole. We can have a lot of squabbles amongst ourselves, but whenever there's salmon being prepared, everybody forgets their differences and eats together. This is something that permeates our tribe and other tribes as well. We remember what's important when we smell that fish cooking over the fire, and we remember what it takes to get it here. We remember that the salmon is also taking quite a journey. It's even more of a journey now than it used to be. It was hard enough then, but now, with technology, habitat problems, pollution, and a lot more fishing out there, it is even more difficult. All of this is what those fish hooks tell me.

Agate Pass, Washington. *Photograph © 2000 Mary Randlett.*

❀ ONGOING CHALLENGES TO FISHING RIGHTS ❀

After decades of bitter struggle in which Indian fishing rights were repeatedly contested, U.S. federal district judge George H. Boldt issued a lengthy opinion in 1974 that reaffirmed Indian fishing rights and guaranteed, among other things, the rights of eligible tribes to half of the harvestable fish each year. The Boldt decision heightened animosity between Indian and non-Indian fishermen and also polarized some tribes, since not all were given the same rights to fish. A positive outgrowth of the Boldt decision has been the establishment of tribal fisheries programs, along with the creation of an intertribal state fisheries commission. At the same time, logging, farming, pollution, dams, and urban development threaten the salmon runs. For the tribes, the loss of salmon is more than an economic and legal problem—it strikes at the heart of their culture.

14 COAST SALISH VOYAGING CANOE

Carrier of the Culture

PEG DEAM

"When the cedar tree comes down, it is transformed into another life-form—a canoe. The canoe carries the people. It carries the songs, the language, the traditional protocol. It carries the salmon, the cattails—everything that's collected. The paddles represent the people who participate and interact with the cedar. It becomes part of the whole culture."

—PEG DEAM

The gift of being chosen

In the old days, it was understood that every newborn child had certain special traits. Elders would watch to see what traits each one had. They would look to see if a child was more interested in carving, hunting, or fishing, in songs, storytelling, or weaving—the whole range

Opposite:
Voyaging canoe model. *Burke Museum collection. Photograph © 1999 Sam Van Fleet.*

Peg Deam. *Photograph © 1999 Mary Randlett.*

Before the establishment of reservations in the 1850s, the greater Puget Sound area was filled with small, permanent villages built on beachfronts or near rivers and streams. During spring and summer, families moved to seasonal fishing and gathering grounds to harvest seafood, berries, roots, and other plants. The yearly cycle alternated between summer camps and the more settled, communal life of the winter villages. The skills necessary to harvest and preserve the abundant natural resources allowed the Coast Salish people to develop a rich social and ceremonial life and to maintain their subsistence. During the winter months, families regrouped in wooden longhouses to prepare for the coming gathering season. They made baskets, carved canoes, and repaired fishnets. Winter was also a time to instruct the children in the ways of their culture, through stories, dance, and song.

Suquamish canoe on beach, ca. 1947. *Photograph by Ernest Bertelson. Courtesy of Special Collections Division, University of Washington Libraries, neg. no. 1617.*

of what was needed to live a day-to-day life. The children were helped along in that area. If there was a fisherman seen in a small child, then the fishermen of the village would teach that child everything they knew. The same with the basket weavers, the hunters—everyone. All children were seen to come with a gift, something that they could contribute in their lifetime.

One of the gifts given to tribal members was being chosen to be a part of, or be allowed to learn, the First Salmon Ceremony. Because we don't have our ancestors' eyes, we can't always pinpoint the gifts of each child today, but there is a way—through dreams. We now have one

tribal member who has dreamed about the First Salmon Ceremony. In acknowledging and encouraging these tribal members to participate and accept their gifts as participants in the First Salmon Ceremony, these things are being brought back to us. They never left—but now we're beginning to develop the vision to see these things again and acknowledge them.

There are tribal members now who could begin doing the ceremony the right way—the way that has been given to us. In a salmon ceremony, the canoe is used together with the cedar boughs and the firewood that cooks the salmon. If we were to have a salmon ceremony

Peg Deam's daughter, Katie Ahvakana, Chief Seattle Days princess. *Photograph © 1995 Ron Peltier.*

again at Suquamish, it would be important to have a cedar canoe that would be brought in ceremonially, carrying the salmon. I can visualize the people participating in the ceremony wearing green cedar boughs and woven cedar bark. When there is something as important as salmon, we can come together and do what's necessary.

Cedar, canoes, and salmon

Cedar, canoes, and salmon are very, very close;

In preparation for the Washington State centennial in 1989, the Native American Canoe Project was organized to rekindle the art of making cedar voyaging canoes, and with it, the skills and stamina required for canoeing. Hundreds of Native people from seventeen western Washington tribes participated in the project. In the summer of 1989, a 170-mile voyage commenced from the Quileute (KWIL-ee-yoot) Reservation along the western Washington coast and culminated in the "Paddle to Seattle"—a dramatic flotilla of thirty canoes that were paddled across the inland Puget Sound from Suquamish to Seattle on July 21, 1989. There, the Washington tribes were met by hundreds of well-wishers, including a Native group from Bella Bella, British Columbia, who extended an invitation to paddle north. Thus was born the modern Northwest Coast canoeing revival, which over time has grown to involve canoeing contacts and voyages between other Canadian tribes and Native Hawaiians.

they have been in the past and they will be in the future. Cedar is one of the primary elements that sustain the culture. It has always been a central element. Every spring, you can count on that cedar having the new bark that furnishes us with materials that we can use in basketry, traditional clothing, and even contemporary cultural art. The green boughs are there for ceremonial uses and healing. The wood itself is there for all of the objects that were used and still are made and used—everything that's carved, including the canoe.

The canoe represents carrying the culture. With the paddles inside, it also represents carrying the people—from the past to the present and into the future. Our traditions say that we have been here since the beginning of time. For thousands of years, hundreds of our villages lined local waterways. We made our living, as many of us still do, from the resources of the sea, the shore, and the forest. We attend gatherings to celebrate our culture. We are rescuing Lushootseed, our Native language, and we are practicing our once-forbidden traditional religion. We are proud of our heritage.

Quileute, Suquamish, and Elwah canoes at Tsyecum, British Columbia. *Photograph © 1993 Ron Peltier.*

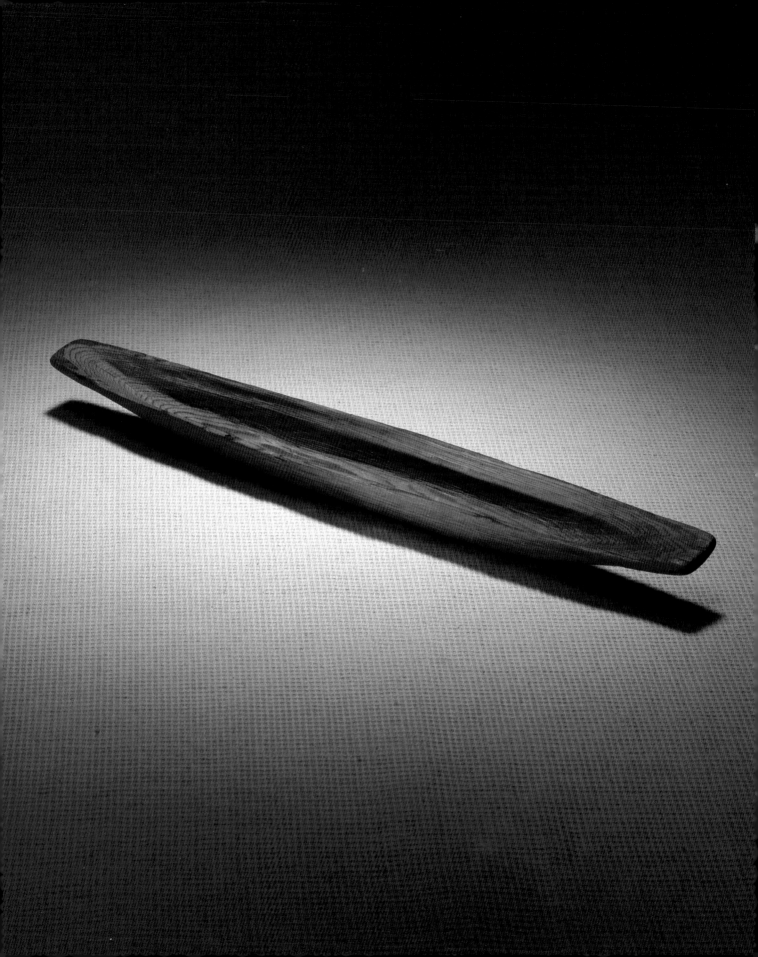

15 COAST SALISH RIVER CANOE

A Place to Learn Patience

VI HILBERT

"We had many canoes for different uses—for lakes or saltwater, for still or rough water. They had different purposes in their designs. The shovel-nosed canoe was used as a river canoe. My dad could make these, and we used them any time we were living near the Skagit River. It was our only transportation. Using a long, limber pole, my dad would push the canoe up crooked places and through rough spots."—VI HILBERT

Opposite:
River canoe model. *Private collection. Photograph © 1999 Sam Van Fleet.*

Vi Hilbert. *Photograph © 2000 Mary Randlett.*

Shovel-nosed canoes for river travel

We lived between Lamon and Hamilton. That was the ancestral land of the Upper Skagit (SKA-jit) people. My dad's people had always lived in that area. There were longhouses side-by-side on the Skagit River. All the spiritual leaders who had large families kept them together in those communal longhouses.

I had some relatives who remembered the Skagit River as a frightful thing that took lives—which it did, often. I never saw it that way though. I always saw the river as a comfortable place to be. Most of the time the river was quite shallow, unless we had winter storms. Living near the river and being with someone who knew the water as well as my dad did helped me feel comfortable. Growing up using the canoes helped me feel that way, too. I knew that the river could be part of the livelihood of my family

and that it could provide a way to travel safely.

The canoes were always made of cedar. We used to have a lot of cedar trees to choose from. Unfortunately, that's no longer true. At the time, my dad was a logger. This was how we had any money in the house. He used his logging tools for our canoes. He'd burn the log to cure it, to seal the wood. Then he'd carve it. The river canoes weren't steamed and spread out at the top like the saltwater ones; they also weren't decorated.

There are still a few people who know how to make these canoes. At least one of my relatives has made a shovel-nosed canoe in the last century. But young people aren't learning to make them now, because the canoes aren't used anymore. The canoeing revival that's occurring is with the saltwater canoes—the big, high canoes that can go through the big waves.

Learning to practice patience

My dad knew all the good fishing places on the river. He had learned from his dad, my grandfather, who had been given the responsibility of identifying which fishing spots were traditional for our people—the Upper Skagit—and which were inherited fishing places for special families.

Fishing with my dad was a quiet time. You had to be completely still. No talking, no moving. It was a time for exercising patience. Looking back, it was a wonderful experience watching him quietly extending that dip net through the water, time and time again, patiently waiting for a salmon to enter that net.

Because I am an only child, my parents knew that in order for our culture to survive and live, they had to instruct me about everything that was important—the things that needed to be remembered. Learning to practice patience with my dad when he was fishing on the river was part of my education.

Vi Hilbert's parents, Louise and Charlie Anderson. *Photographs © 1956 Virginia Mohling. Courtesy of Vi Hilbert.*

Many of the threads that tied together traditional Coast Salish culture—including the Suquamish and Upper Skagit tribes—began to fray with the establishment of reservations in the wake of the treaties negotiated between the U.S. government and Northwest tribes in 1854 and 1855. Not only were vast tracts of land taken away from the Native people, but children were forcibly taken away from their homes and sent to boarding schools. There, they were taught the ways of a foreign culture and forbidden to speak their own languages. When they returned home, they had missed the long months of traditional instruction from their elders. Many ceremonies, including the First Salmon Ceremony, were forbidden and many skills were lost as different materials and ways of doing things were introduced. Efforts to revive Native languages and cultural practices began during the civil rights movement of the 1960s. While this was too late for some things to be recovered, it provided an important spark for today's resurgence of cultural pride and accomplishment.

We're taught from childhood never to ask questions. So I observed, but I did not ask questions. I had to be bright enough to use my eyes and use deduction to find the answers. My cousin, who was very, very traditional, said that if you have to ask questions, you're too dumb to learn. I didn't want to be considered stupid, so I never asked questions. On the other hand, in *this* culture, you're considered stupid if you don't ask questions!

Passing on culture through rituals

So much of our culture has been lost because the people who remembered were not able to pass on their information. Children were sent away to boarding schools, and traditional ways were discouraged. Even our language was forbidden. At one time, every river group had its own special salmon ceremony honoring the spirit of the first salmon caught of the season. With the establishment of the reservations, these practices became dormant for a hundred years. They were only revived on the Skagit by my uncle and my cousin in the 1970s. My grandfather had been the head man on the Skagit in his time, and different members of my family knew a lot about the First Salmon Ceremony.

Because the salmon played such a central role in the lives of the Pacific Northwest peoples, the spirit of the first salmon caught of the season was always honored. At each location, there were slightly different ways of approaching the ceremony. The Lummis were the only people who bit off the tiny fin that's back by the tail. The person who told me this was worried that no one would remember this detail after she was gone.

Practicing these ceremonies is a very important part of the culture. It is through rituals that we remind our young people of what is important. When elders who can pass on this information cease to exist, the world is going to be in trouble. But as long as traditional people make it their business to pass on the importance of these rituals, the world itself, not only our people, will be the richer for it.

First Salmon Ceremony at Village Point, Lummi Island, ca. 1910. *Photograph courtesy of Lummi Archives, accession no. AC268P1.*

16 NORTHWEST COAST WOLF HEADDRESS

Representation of Who We Are

GEORGE DAVID

"The wolf headdress represents who we are. Our winter ceremony is a wolf ceremony called Tlookwana. That identifies my people, meaning not just the Nuu-chah-nulth tribe, but my family. You might hear other people say, "We are Raven, we are Eagle, we are Killer Whale clan." Me, I'm Tlookwana, that's the house I come from. It's not just a family crest, it's who we are. It's our power, our identity with nature and everything that's around us. The wolf is our closest brother. We have songs that call the wolves down from the hills—not just physically, but their spiritual presence. When we sing those songs, the wolves come. They are with us, whether we're here in Seattle or in our homeland on the west coast of Vancouver Island."—GEORGE DAVID

George David. *Photograph © 2000 Mary Randlett.*

Opposite:
Makah wolf headdress, late nineteenth century. *Burke Museum collection. Photograph © 1987 Ray Fowler.*

Opitsaht Village. *Photograph courtesy of the Royal British Columbia Museum, Victoria, British Columbia, neg. no. PN17784.*

When wolves come to the village

I don't have personal memories of the winter ceremony going on in my village, but I know it through my brothers' memories and their stories. If my parents didn't go to the community hall and participate in the winter ceremony, they stayed in the house with us and made sure we behaved. They put blankets over the windows and doors. We couldn't peek outside when the wolves came from the community hall and went around through the village. All the parents who stayed in the houses would tell their kids, "You better behave, the wolves are here. If you're not going to behave, we're going to take you and throw you out the door. They're going to take you away." And they would! That was part of the wolf ritual.

The wolves are mythological beings whose spirits came down to the village. Their power was with the people who were wearing the wolf headdresses and blowing those big whistles. If children were put outside, those men wearing the wolf headdresses and blankets grabbed the children and brought them back to the community hall. They kept them there for four days, separated from their parents. They did ceremonies with them—not really praying, but a ceremonial part of prayer. When the children were returned to their parents, they wouldn't talk about what had happened. It was part of the ceremony, an aspect of learning. They behaved and they tried to be better people—young people, but better people.

All of this is part of my recollection of the wolf headdress, including the carving and the shaping of the wood. I know all that because I'm an artist and carver. But the actual use of a wolf headdress is very, very sacred. It's very powerful, very strong. I can't describe all of it because it's a closed ceremony, a secret society. The old people said it's nothing to play around with. It's not a matter-of-fact thing. It's a very serious part of our society.

Becoming the wolf

The masks weren't on display in our houses. They weren't on the counter. They weren't in a glass case. They were wrapped up properly and put away in a box unless we were doing a ceremony or a dance. Even the wolf headdresses that were used for dancing in the home were kept wrapped up in a box and stored behind a dance curtain.

George David wearing the Burke Museum's wolf headdress, 2000. *Line drawing by Paula Chandler David.*

From when I was very young, my dad used to tell me, "A wolf headdress, a mask, and everything you dance with, you don't put it on until just before you're going to step out onto the floor when that song starts and you dance that dance. If it's a wolf, you don't go out there and try to make like a wolf; you don't try to imitate them. Instead, you *become* that wolf. If you can't do that, don't step out on the floor." That's how serious it was.

When you're through dancing and come behind the curtain, you take the headdress off. You put it away where nobody else can touch or look at it. That's the way it is, because you *transform*, you become that wolf—or whatever it is you're dancing—when you dance. I've understood that since I was really young.

Carrying on traditions away from home

I lived on the west coast of Vancouver Island in a little village called Opitsaht until I was seven. Out of thirteen children, I was the last born. Six girls, seven boys. Now there are five of us left.

In 1956, when I was six, we came down to Seattle for the summer and returned north that fall. The following year we all came down for good. My father was ill—he had some kind of rheumatism—and we were looking for a warmer climate. We kept moving farther and farther south, and finally settled in Yuma, Arizona. In 1959, we moved back to the Seattle area, liking it the most. There was a lot of water and it was on the West Coast. Yuma is very dry. It was good for my father when he was ill, but we were homesick for the Northwest and were happy to move back to the Seattle area.

❀ TILLICUM VILLAGE ❀

Tillicum Village is located on Blake Island, a Washington State park located thirty minutes by boat from Seattle. It opened in 1962—the year of the Seattle World's Fair—as the sole concession on the island. It continues operation today as a tourist venue offering cultural dinner theater based on Northwest Coast Indian heritage. The idea for Tillicum Village (which means "friendly village") grew from founder Bill Hewitt's hobby of cooking salmon in the traditional Indian way—the fish is split lengthwise and barbecued on cedar skewers in front of a hot fire. From the establishment's earliest days, Hewitt hired local Indian people to barbecue salmon, demonstrate carving and other crafts, and perform dances during dinner.

Tillicum Village on Blake Island, Washington, 1997.
Photograph by Kevin Morris.

Winnefred David barbecuing salmon at Tillicum Village.
Photograph courtesy of Mark Hewett.

We had been in Seattle for three years when Bill Hewitt knocked on our door. He was developing Tillicum Village on Blake Island in Puget Sound. He was putting together a group of Native people who could bake salmon and perform, and who knew enough about their cultural history to talk to visitors who came to Blake Island to see a bit of Indian culture.

Everywhere Hewitt went, he heard my father's name. My father was a historian and knew quite a bit about everything. So Hewitt came out and talked to my father and asked him if he actually did know a lot about the stories and songs and so on. My father said yes. Hewitt asked if his children danced, and my father said yes. When he asked my mother if she knew how to barbecue salmon and she said yes, Hewitt knew he had a family that could do a lot of things he wanted done over there. So he hired us and we went to Blake Island for the summer.

The children—my brothers and I—danced

and my father sang. My father was also the resident carver and my mother barbecued the salmon. It was quite a summer! After that, we didn't all go back to Blake Island together. But my parents, my brother Hyacinth, and I went for a couple years. We returned year after year. That was the beginning of our interest in becoming artists.

Blake Island and Tillicum Village have always been nice things to reflect back on. Hyacinth and I are internationally known artists now, and in 1998 we carved a totem pole at Tillicum Village commemorating my father, whom we lost in 1976. Our mother was eighty-eight when we dedicated the pole. The wolf was a central figure on the totem pole because Tlookwana—that's our ceremony.

The meaning behind the art

The most important part of an artifact is what it is used for. What *is* that mask? What does it *really* mean? The meaning of the art is the most important—where it all comes from.

We all know what a wolf is or what a bird is. But what does a thunderbird mean to the Nuu-chah-nulth (NOO-CHAH-noolth) people? Where did it come from? Why is it so important? To answer that, you have to go back to the process of obtaining a dance, a mask, a song, a story—it is very rigorous. It's something on the level of a vision quest, going out into nature for something that's going to help you.

All of our people did that when we reached the age of maturity—anywhere between fifteen and eighteen. There was a time when we were sent out into the woods for four days. You wouldn't take water and you wouldn't eat. You were fasting, praying, and seeking what you were going to be as a grown man or grown woman. During that time, some people obtained dances, headdresses, masks, and songs to go with them. It's quite a process. It's not as easy as one might think. It's something that was sought after, but not too many people got it.

When something was gifted to a person, that's what it was—a gift from the spirits. When the person returned to the village, this gift would be celebrated. The person would be taken care of upon reentering the village. They would be fed and the ceremony would continue. They would bring out what was obtained and celebrate it.

❋ WINTER CEREMONIES—THE WOLF RITUAL ❋

The wolf ritual, Tlookwana (TLOOK-wah-nah), was historically the most important winter ceremony practiced by the Nuu-chah-nulth people. It continues to be performed by initiated members of the wolf society and involves the seizing and initiating of others. Tlookwana was traditionally sponsored by a wealthy chief to initiate a son or other young relative. It could last for up to two weeks and was accompanied by feasting and potlatching as well as the use of masks, headdresses, and other props; theatrical performance; and comic entertainment. Practice of the wolf ritual had nearly disappeared by the 1970s, and many Nuu-chah-nulth remembered it only from their childhood or from the stories of their elders. It has slowly revived since then, and people are once again being initiated into the secret society. George David and his brothers have been initiated, as have others involved in the cultural revival occurring all along the Northwest Coast.

No matter what it was—information, a song, medicine, a dance.

Earning the rights to family privileges

There can be a lot of family history about particular dances and songs. For example, there's a white wolf dance within a branch of my family. Once, when a young man from that branch of the family was out in the woods, late in the evening on his fourth day, he saw two white wolves running in a clearing. They were fast, lightning fast. He obtained a dance and a song from those white wolves. He grabbed one of them and the wolf said, "Watch!" and he showed him a dance. And then the wolf said, "Listen!" and he sang a song. When the young man came back to the village, he brought those things with him. They were gifts. That's where our art, our dances, our songs—everything we are as a people—come from.

The right to use these songs and dances is passed along within a family. If it goes further than that, then it's potlatched. The *right* is given, not the dance. In the potlatch system, anything we own goes down from father to oldest living son. The overseeing of songs, dances, names—everything that's passed on—goes through the oldest son. He doesn't own them alone; he's just the overseer. I, as the youngest male in my family, have the right to dance what our family owns, but I can't do it unless I go to my oldest brother and ask him. What I would say is, "I want to do this. Can I use this song? Can I do this dance?" His responsibility is to keep everything straight and proper. He'll more than likely say yes. If he says no, it's usually for a very good reason.

When you stand up in the front of a community hall or longhouse and talk to the people and sing the songs, you have to know exactly how you acquired the right to sing that song or use that mask. You explain it all, either before or after you do it. That's the way it's structured. This has been extended to sisters or daughters. Now there are other things that women are just as responsible for. It's not all through the male anymore.

❁ POTLATCHING ON THE NORTHWEST COAST ❁

Potlatches, which occur all along the Northwest Coast, are formal ceremonies to commemorate an important event, such as a wedding, a memorial, or the bestowal of an inherited family name. Potlatches allow high-ranking chiefs to reaffirm their status through the public display of inherited privileges. These might include the right to use certain songs or dances, or the right to display family crests such as Killer Whale or Wolf. Guests to a potlatch serve as formal witnesses to the event and receive gifts as payment for their presence. By the time potlatches were first witnessed by outsiders in the mid-1800s, they included feasting, dancing, singing, formal speeches, and the display and distribution of large quantities of goods. This emphasis on material accumulation and the performance of highly theatrical dances shocked early missionaries and led the Canadian government to outlaw potlatches in 1885. In spite of the ban, potlatches continued to be carried on in private (similar to hula among Native Hawaiians), especially in remote villages. The ban on potlatches was rescinded in 1951, and since then potlatches have been held with increasing frequency all along the Northwest Coast.

Northwest Coast Indian art is renowned for its beauty, design complexity, and rich symbolic meaning. The great artists of the past were respected community members who were not only gifted with the tools of their craft but carried with them a deep knowledge of the cultural traditions from which their art derived. Northwest Coast artists continue to be respected as carriers of tradition today. They have been deeply involved with the renaissance of Northwest Coast cultural practices and have led the revival of associated material culture such as masks, button blankets, jewelry, and monumental carvings like house posts, totem poles, and canoes.

A carving style that stresses character

I've made numerous wolf headdresses in different tribal styles, not only Nuu-chah-nulth. I've done Tlingit (tling-GIT) and some of the other styles. When I started doing art work, I wanted to know as much as possible, so I started up north, with the Tsimshian (sim-see-AHN) style, and moved on down south to Nuu-chah-nulth, which is my tribal identity.

I've worked with museum collections, slides, and books. But, as much as possible, I try to work with other people who were educated in different styles. My older brother, Hyacinth, carved long before I did and knew quite a bit. I've learned a lot from him. I also learned by teaching myself and working with other people. I owe a lot of gratitude to the people who gave me their time as I went along. I eventually got to the point where I was comfortable and knew enough that I could design in the different styles but not do the old designs. Then it became art; it became my art.

The Nuu-chah-nulth wolf may look simpler than the more heavily carved or painted northern wolf headdress, but it has a strength of character in that seeming simplicity. Our carving style is like that. We try not to bring attention to too many details, too much ornamentation. We're trying to hear the voice of the wolf. It is simpler, but more intense. When we're carving, our train of thought is towards the power of what's going on. Our art comes from ceremony, not the other way around.

Because we're artists, we work with galleries. I've probably made thirty or forty wolf masks. I don't do the same thing every time. When I sit down to make one, even if it's very similar to one I've made before, there's always that push, that twist, to make it a little different. I can look at what I'm producing and see growth and development both in my own art and in the boundaries of Nuu-chah-nulth art. We get critical comments sometimes, if we go too far out of bounds of what has been done before and of what is expected. We try to stay within the boundaries of our traditions. But as artists, we also try to push the borderlines a little bit, too. As Nuu-chah-nulth people, we're always responsible for what we say, what we do, what we carve—always. I think of all these things when I look at the wolf headdress and when I'm making one.

17 IÑUPIAQ *UMIAQ*

Symbol of a Way of Life

LARRY ULAAQ AHVAKANA

"The umiaq *is a key to understanding who the Iñupiat people are. It's an integral part of the culture."*—LARRY ULAAQ AHVAKANA

An open boat for travel and whaling

The *umiaq* (oo-mee-yahk) is an open boat, eighteen to twenty-four feet long. It's made out of driftwood and is covered with skins from bearded seals (*ugruk*) (oog-rook). It usually takes about five to six skins to cover an *umiaq*. Women sew the skins together in a special way so that they won't leak. My grandmother sewed a lot of *umiaqs* in her time.

Opposite:
Umiaq model, late 1800s, Point Barrow, Alaska.
Burke Museum collection. Photograph © 1999 Sam Van Fleet.

Larry Ahvakana. *Photograph © 1999 Mary Randlett.*

Uncovered *umiaq* frame in Barrow, Alaska, 2000. *Photograph by Edward Liebow.*

Umiaq with skin cover, Barrow, Alaska, 2000. *Photograph by Edward Liebow.*

Umiaqs are still made with skins today. More than half of the whaling crews still use skin boats. Long ago, putting the skins on was part of the ceremonial activity associated with whaling. Sometimes, new skins were put on every year. Now, people may keep the skins on for three or four years.

Usually, after the skins are used, the women cut them up and pass them out to different people for making *mukluks* (shoes), tunics, boots, and other things. The recycling of material is very important to the Iñupiat (in-YOOP-yaht). When the women make things for the whalers, it adds to the feeling of continuity with the past, of being part of another boat that has hunted whales. When we catch a whale, there are a lot of good spirits associated with that skin. When the skins are reused by hunters, it helps provide luck for future hunts.

Unlike the skins, the wood frames of the *umiaqs* are kept until they wear out, maybe ten or twenty years. To keep the wood from rotting, the *umiaqs* are put up on scaffolding in the winter. You can see them in the village, with or without the skins on.

Umiaqs are used for travel and for whaling. I can remember going out to a place called Near the Point when I was a little boy. We'd go there in our *umiaqs* to hunt ducks and geese. Once we got there, we camped out. Usually we paddled the *umiaqs*, but sometimes motors were strapped on to the boats. In the past, people also used sails. My parents have told me that they sometimes used sails with masts when they went out hunting walrus, which are usually out on the ice floes, over the deeper water. If they had gone out with the current, it could be hard to paddle back over the long distances, so they used sails to get back to the village.

Going back to Barrow

I was born in Fairbanks, Alaska, and moved to Barrow when I was very young. We lived there

The Iñupiat—formerly known as Alaskan Eskimos—have traditionally been coastal whalers, working from the shore and at the edge of the ice to take bowhead whales as they come in to feed. Farther south, whaling tribes like the Nuu-chah-nulth and Makah were seafaring whalers who pursued migrating gray and humpback whales in canoes through open waters. Until recently, the Iñupiat were the only indigenous group allowed to continue whaling for subsistence purposes. Overhunting by commercial whalers at the turn of the century led to an international ban on whaling to protect the dwindling whale populations. In 1998, the Makah, who live on the northwestern tip of Washington State, were granted permission to resume limited hunting of gray whales for subsistence. In May 1999, they took their first whale in over eighty years. Iñupiat whalers and other Native people traveled from throughout the Northwest to acknowledge the Makah and participate in the ceremonial distribution of whale meat.

until I was seven. Then my family moved to Anchorage. At that point I didn't understand how to speak English very well. Having that early experience of living in the village helped me keep alive the feeling of wanting to understand more of my culture. But because I left Barrow when I was seven and spent my school years elsewhere, I didn't have an opportunity to experience the Iñupiat way of life through language or other experiences until I went back to Barrow as an adult to be a part of a whaling crew.

My father was an *umialik* (oo-mee-ah-lik), a whaling captain. I was fortunate to be able to go out with him and my grandfather, and also my uncles and other relatives. That opportunity to go whaling really cemented the idea of who I was—who I am—and my place within my community and the Iñupiat people. It helped me to put aside a lot of the confused and antagonistic ideas I had about being Iñupiaq and growing up in an urban environment.

I was thirty when I went whaling, so it took a long time for the circle to come back around again, to be part of the village and the ceremonial aspect of living there. Going whaling made me feel like a part of Iñupiat life. The experience was also a unique opportunity for me to get more in touch with the material side of the culture—the whaling implements, the *umiaq*. The dances and songs and ceremonies also became more understandable to me. Going back helped me to understand a bit more about the whaling festival I remembered from when I was little. The experience stirred up memories of better times—times I had spent with my grandparents, and the feasting after the whale hunt.

After that first hunt, I went back to Barrow for several years to go whaling. The last year I went, we caught the whale. That was really a dramatic feeling. It was the last time our family went out whaling together. It was a very important time in our family history.

A sculptural representation of whaling culture

Coming from a family that worked in art also helped me get closer to my cultural identity. Understanding the material things and how to make them helped me understand what it means to be Iñupiaq. These things have become a driving force behind my own art.

The sculpture I made for the "Pacific Voices" exhibit at the Burke Museum ties many of these ideas together. It's actually a model for a full-size bronze sculpture I plan to make for the cultural center in Barrow. It depicts a harpooner poised to strike a bowhead whale, which has surfaced in a lead (an opening) in the ice. It's the last chance the harpooner has to hit the whale that season. Under international whaling treaties, each crew gets only a limited number of chances to take a whale.

The sculpture is realistic, but the figures are symbolic. The steersman in the back of the *umiaq* represents the old traditions. He guides the people in the practices of whaling and symbolizes continuity with the past. The man who wears the loon headdress represents the shaman who calls away the spirits of the whales, cleansing the hunters of any trace of earlier hunts. He would not actually be in the *umiaq* but symbolizes the ceremonial preparation for the hunt. The young man on the left side is participating

in his first hunt and represents the passing on of the traditions. Next to him is a woman who inherited her right to whale from her husband. Such women have participated in whaling since at least the late nineteenth century. The harpooner, who stands at the front of the *umiaq*, is using a modern weapon to hit the whale—a harpoon with a detachable head and explosive charge. The *umiaq* itself carries the crew to the whale and, like the steersman, represents continuity with the past.

Preparing for the hunt

The *agviq* (AHG-vik) (bowhead whale) is more than a sustaining food for our people. It is a strong source of our cultural identity. We think of ourselves as part of the whale. Part of the preparation for the whale hunt is getting things ready in winter. Men get the gear ready. Women make new clothes and sew the *umiaq* covers. It is also a time for the winter ceremony, a time to appease the spirits. It's when we pass out the rest of the whale meat that has been stored over the winter. We clear out the ice cellars. In doing that, the souls of the whales and other animals that have been caught during the year are given up and sent back home. When we catch the whale, its spirit goes inside us, and if we don't have the ceremony to take the spirit away, the new whales that come will recognize their relatives and won't come close to us.

The whaling captain has a very important role. He is the leader of the whaling ceremonies. He's the one who passes on the traditions through song and dance, and through the activities surrounding the hunt. To become an

Last Chance, **Larry Ahvakana, 1996, sculpture.** *Burke Museum collection. Photograph © 1999 by Sam Van Fleet.*

umialik, the person should come from a lineage of whalers. The implements for whaling are passed on from father to son: the *umiaq*, the tools for whaling. The *umialik* also has to have the money, food, and material to put a whaling crew together.

Waiting for *agviq* to come

We don't go and chase the whales; we wait for them to come to us. We have our camp next to that lead opening. We set the *umiaq* out on the ice, not in the water. It's placed where we can shove it into the water when we see the whale come near. Then we float near where the whale might come back up.

Long ago, Iñupiat people used to carry small objects that they would tie onto the *umiaqs* for good luck in the whale hunt. They also carved prow ornaments with a whale image. These could be used as a seat or placed up front to hold the coiled line and harpoon. The image of the whale would face down over the water so only the whale could see it. With the introduction of Christianity, things like that were prohibited. The missionaries thought they were demonic, so we stopped making them.

Honoring the whale

As soon as a whale is pulled up onto the ice, it is given fresh water to "drink." Since the whale lives in saltwater, this is the first and last time it can drink fresh water. The fresh water soothes its thirst. Afterwards, its spirit can go on its journey.

The whale is cut up in a traditional way, and

Blanket toss. *Photograph © 1990 Bill Hess.*

portions are given out. The effort is very intense. There may be two hundred or three hundred people working on it. It has to be done right after the whale has been caught, because there's a lot of heat within the whale and the meat spoils quickly. As the pieces are cut up, they are distributed in a prescribed order: to the whaling captain, to the crews, to the villagers, and then to everyone else.

The whale feast is the culminating part of the whale festival. The "blanket toss" is part of the festival and is a way to honor the whale and

the people who caught it. The *umiaqs* are part of this, too. Because it is often windy, the *umiaqs* are pulled up onto the ice and set on their sides to make a windbreak. People sit under them for shelter. The skins are cut off an old *umiaq* and used as a blanket to toss the people up. The whaling crew is thrown up in the air first, one at a time. When you are up in the air, you can look into the mountains, where the whale's spirit is going. Then you turn around and look out to the ocean. This appeases the spirit of the whale, telling it that you are part of its society and that you have taken it and eaten it to survive—not just to hunt it and kill it.

An enduring symbol

The *umiaq* is a very practical thing, a useful mode of transportation. It is also an enduring symbol of our Iñupiat way of life. It's especially close to whaling, which is our most important traditional activity. Whaling is integral to who we are as a people.

The *umiaq* also symbolizes our sovereignty, that we have a specific way of life even though we live within another governmental system. Nothing will deprive us of that source of energy and power. We still carry on the traditions of a subsistence lifestyle. We still have the ability to make *umiaqs*, to collect the skins, to do traditional whaling.

We've built a new cultural center in Bar-

Barrow Cultural Center, 2000. *Photograph by Edward Liebow.*

Larry Ahvakana working with clay models. *Photograph © 1999 Mary Randlett.*

row. Within it, we have a space where people can learn to make *umiaqs*. Elders teach younger people how to make the traditional implements of hunting and, especially, whaling. So this knowledge will be carried on. If anything, the *umiaq* will have an even bigger role in our understanding of our culture. It's a true expression of it. For people like myself, who don't live in our home communities anymore, the ability to retain our cultural identity is strengthened through an understanding of cultural materials like the *umiaq*.

Opposite above:
Umiaq on the edge of the water. *Photograph © 1998 Bill Hess.*

Opposite below:
Crew pursuing the whale. *Photograph © 1998 Bill Hess.*

CONCLUSION

Voices Within Our Community

ERIN YOUNGER

T HE "VOICES" HEARD WITHIN THE
pages of this book belong to people linked
to one another in the broadest terms by
their Pacific Rim origins. Some were born and
raised in Washington State; others came from
Canada or arrived as war refugees or immigrants
from overseas. Today they live as neighbors,
making up a small but representative sample of
the broad mix that has come to be understood as
cultural diversity in the United States. As individuals, they came to know one another through
their work on the Burke Museum's "Pacific
Voices" exhibit. Through that experience, they
shared what they had in common, discussed
what their cultural heritage meant to them, and
grappled with how best to communicate its
importance to others.

When they were asked to choose a single

Opposite:
**Choonyang Lee hits the big
drum for New York's Soh Daiko.**
*Photograph © Lauren
Greenfield.*

Erin Younger and Miriam Kahn.
*Photograph
© 2005 Mary Randlett.*

object to discuss for this book, they made their selections with little hesitation. For some, the associations were tinged with sadness and loss; for others, the objects connected vividly to a sense of ongoing cultural engagement and revival. While the details are personal and varied, the discussions are linked by the narrators' shared sense of the resonance of cultural identity. In the search for personal identity, they turned to the language and stories with which they had grown up, the wisdom and teaching of their elders, and the shared celebrations of community they had experienced in their lives.

When viewed as a group, the objects are remarkably different from one another. What do canoes and a headdress have in common? How are incense burners and feather cloaks related? They are made of different materials and used in dissimilar ways. Some have been passed on for generations; others are crafted anew. Some take years of training to learn how to make; others can be purchased in a store. Some are hard to transport; others fit comfortably in an airplane's overhead compartment. Yet, each of the objects has a capacity to trigger deeply felt memories and to instill a sense of continued cultural connection. For George David, for example, the wolf headdress is much more than an object to carve and wear on his forehead. It represents the essence of who he is and the traditional knowledge required to be Nuu-chah-nulth.

For many, what is most important is that the objects are still used. It doesn't matter, for example, if a Vietnamese family home has a large, inlaid cabinet or a small, simple shelf for the ancestor altar. What matters is that it holds an incense burner and is used daily as a place to pray. For others, the process of making the object is as important as the act of using it. 'Iwalani Christian and Moodette Ka'apana studied hula for years before each was ready to make her first *pahu*. They took seriously the challenge of finding the right tree, determining the appropriate design, and selecting a proper name for their drums. Buying the drum was out of the question; making their own was an essential step in becoming a hula master.

When the chosen object represents a way of life that can no longer be followed, the feeling it triggers is often one of nostalgia. Yet, even when cultural traditions are no longer practiced, the ability to think and talk about them is useful. Sapina Pele noted that, while it is very hard to convey the full meaning of the wooden *tānoa* bowl when it sits on a table in her living room in Seattle rather than in front of a chief at a feast in Samoa, it can nonetheless stimulate conversation. When she places her small *tānoa* on her desk at the school where she works, it sparks conversations with Samoan students about their heritage. Similarly, Sonia Kim views the Korean gourd cups as symbols of a past way of life—of the good and bad sons, Heungbu and Nolbu—which have no ready equivalent in Seattle but remind her of how to behave according to Korean values, no matter where she lives.

The power of special objects is such that they always command the attention and respect of their guardians. Those who carry the knowledge of what the objects mean, and how they are used, help to keep the knowledge alive. All the contributors to this book acknowledge that this is no easy task. Yet they feel strongly that young people, especially, need a place to which they can go that is rich in cultural values. The lives of many who grew up embraced by cultural traditions have, in fact, been changed abruptly— by economics, war, a family move, or personal choice—causing them to leave their roots behind. Yet, years later, each has come back to reclaim some portion of his or her cultural heritage, using it as a means of defining personal identity and connecting to a broader community. Larry Ahvakana, for example, left the Iñupiat village of Barrow early in his life, only to come full circle and rejoin it as a young adult. For him, the experience of whaling cemented his sense of connection with his ancestors and helped him understand who he is and how to celebrate his Iñupiat heritage in both his art and his lifestyle. Others, born in the United States, may travel widely in search of their roots. For the members of Seattle Matsuri Taiko, traveling to Japan is one of the goals and rewards of playing *taiko* with the group. While in Japan, they not only steep themselves in Japanese culture, but they also visit stores with *taiko* materials and drums, which are on their wish list of items that help them connect with their heritage.

The need to understand one's roots and one's place in the world is universal. Individuals have always looked back to reaffirm their ties with the past and gain insights for the future. Stories are remembered, recounted, and transformed. Ceremonies are revived, performed, and reinvented. Special objects imbued with significance are a part of this process and experience. Like hope chests for the future, these "objects of culture" are taken along on life's voyages no matter where one goes. They may be carried across borders and refashioned from new materials. They may be hung on a wall or put on a table. They may be used every day or kept as a treasured memory. Wherever they are found—as the images and stories in this book convey—they represent the creative cultural vitality that exists in the many voices within each of our communities.

SUGGESTED READING

GENERAL

Pelz, Ruth, ed.
1998   *Pacific Voices: Celebrating the Worlds within Our Community.* Exhibit guide. Seattle: The Burke Museum of Natural History and Culture.

1 & 2 HAWAIIAN *PAHU*

Beamer, Nona
1987   *A Collection of Hawaiian Hula Chants.* Vol. 1 of *Na Mele Hula.* Honolulu: University of Hawai'i Press.
2002   *Hawaiian Hula Rituals and Chants.* Vol. 2 of *Na Mele Hula.* Honolulu: University of Hawai'i Press.

Buck, Peter
1964   *Musical Instruments.* Vol. 9 of *Arts and Crafts of Hawai'i.* Special publication 45. Honolulu: Bishop Museum.

Emerson, Nathaniel B.
1965   *Unwritten Literature of Hawai'i: The Sacred Songs of the Hula.* Tokyo: Charles E. Tuttle Company.

Kaeppler, Adrienne
1980   *Pahu and Puniu: An Exhibition of Hawaiian Drums.* Honolulu: Bishop Museum.

1993a   *Ha'a and Hula Pahu: Sacred Movements.* Vol. 1 of *Hula Pahu: Hawaiian Drum Dances.* Honolulu: Bishop Museum.
1993b   *The Pahu: Sounds of Power.* Vol. 2 of *Hula Pahu: Hawaiian Drum Dances.* Honolulu: Bishop Museum.

Tatar, Elizabeth
1987   *Strains of Change: The Impact of Tourism on Hawaiian Music.* Honolulu: Bishop Museum.

3 SAMOAN *TĀNOA*

Amituana'i, Tevita
1986   "Kava in Samoa." *Pacific Rituals.* Honolulu: Institute of Pacific Studies.

Lebot, Vincent, Mark Merlin, and Lamont Lindstrom
1992   *Kava: The Pacific Drug.* New Haven, CT: Yale University Press.

Malauulu, J.
1974   "Kava: Legends, Ceremony, How to Make and Serve It." *Faasamoa Pea* 1 (2): 20–37.

Thomas, Nicholas
1991   *Entangled Objects: Exchange, Material Culture, and Colonialism in the Pacific.* Cambridge, MA: Harvard University Press.

4 MAORI *KOROWAI*

Mead, Hirini Moko
1968 *Te Whatu Taaniko / Taaniko Weaving.* Auckland: Reed Methuen.
1969 *Traditional Maori Clothing.* Wellington: AH and AW Reed.

Pendergrast, Mick
1984 *Feathers and Fibre: A Survey of Traditional and Contemporary Maori Craft.* Auckland: Rutura Art Gallery.
1987 *Te Aho Tapu / The Sacred Thread: Traditional Maori Weaving.* Honolulu: University of Hawai'i Press.
1997 *Kakahu / Maori Cloaks.* Auckland: David Bateman Ltd.

Puketapu-Hetet, Erenora
1989 *Maori Weaving.* Auckland: Pitman.

Te Kanawa, Diggeress
1992 *Weaving a Kakahu.* Wellington: Bridget Williams Books.

5 MICRONESIAN CANOE

Ashby, Gene, ed.
1993 *Some Things of Value: Micronesian Customs and Beliefs.* Eugene, OR: Rainy Day Press.

Feldman, Jerome, and Donald H. Rubenstein
1986 *Art of Micronesia.* Honolulu: University of Hawai'i Art Gallery.

Gladwin, Thomas
1970 *East Is a Big Bird: Navigation and Logic on Puluwat Atoll.* Cambridge, MA: Harvard University Press.

Haddon, A. C., and James Hornell
1975 *Canoes of Oceania.* Honolulu: Bishop Museum.

Kane, Herb Kawainui
1993 "The Seekers." *Manoa* 5 (1).

Kyselka, Will
1987 *An Ocean in Mind.* Honolulu: University of Hawai'i Press.

Lewis, David
1972 *We, the Navigators: The Ancient Art of Landfinding in the Pacific.* Honolulu: University of Hawai'i Press.

Montuel-Cohen, M.
1987 *Continuity and Change in the Material Culture of Micronesia.* Mangiloo: Isla Center for the Arts at the University of Guam.

Thomas, Stephen
1987 *The Last Navigator.* Camden, ME: McGraw-Hill.

Wavell, Barbara B.
1996 *The Art of Micronesia.* Exhibition catalogue. Maitland, FL: Maitland Art Center.

6 VIETNAMESE INCENSE BURNER

Elliot, Duong Van Mai
2000 *The Sacred Willow: Four Generations in the Life of a Vietnamese Family.* Oxford: Oxford University Press.

Ellis, Claire
1995 *Culture Shock! Vietnam.* Portland, OR: Graphic Arts Center Publishing Company.

Hayslip, Le Ly
1994 *When Heaven and Earth Changed Places.* London: Pan Books.

Jamieson, Neil L.
1995 *Understanding Vietnam.* Los Angeles: University of California Press.

Lewis, Norman
1982 *A Dragon Apparent: Travels in Cambodia, Laos and Vietnam.* London: Eland.

McLeod, Mark W., and Nguyen Thi Dieu
2001 *Culture and Customs of Vietnam.* Westport, CT: Greenwood.

Templer, Robert
1999 *Shadows and Wind: A View of Modern Vietnam.* London: Penguin.

7 LAO *KHAEN*

Catlin, Amy
1992 *Text, Context, and Performance in Cambodia, Laos, and Vietnam.* Vol. 9 of *Selected Reports in Ethnomusicology.* Los Angeles: University of California.

Clewley, John
2000 "Beyond Our Khaen" in *Latin & North America, Caribbean, India, Asia and Pacific*. Vol. 2 of *World Music*, 170–74. London: Rough Guides Ltd., Penguin.

Lee, Yuan-Yuan, and Shen Sin-Yan
1999 *Chinese Musical Instruments*. Woodridge, IL: Chinese Music Society of North America.

Miller, Terry E.
1991 *Introduction to Playing the Khaen*. Kent, OH: World Music Enterprises.

Miller, Terry E., and Jarernchai Chonpairot
1994 "A History of Siamese Music Reconstructed from Western Documents, 1505–1932." *Crossroads* 8 (2): 1–192.

Thrasher, Alan R.
2001 *Chinese Musical Instruments*. Oxford: Oxford University Press.

Yupho, Dhanit
1987 *Thai Musical Instruments*. Bangkok: Krom Sinlap̄akͅon.

8 PHILIPPINE SANTO NIÑO

Canella, Fenella
1999 *Power and Intimacy in the Christian Philippines*. New York: Cambridge University Press.

Galende, Pedro G., and Rene B. Javellana
1993 *Great Churches of the Philippines*. Manila: Bookmark, Inc.

Hornedo, Florentino H.
2000 *Culture and Community in the Philippine Fiesta and Other Celebrations*. Manila: Santo Tomas University.

Mulder, Niels
2000 *Filipino Images: Culture of the Public World*. Quezon City, Philippines: New Day.

Ness, Sally Ann
1987 *The Sinulog Dancing of Cebu City, Philippines: A Semiotic Analysis*. Ph.D. diss. University of Washington, Seattle.

Rodell, Paul A.
2002a *Culture and Customs of the Philippines*. Westport, CT: Greenwood.
2002b *Santo Niño: The Holy Child Devotion in the Philippines*. Manila: Congregacion del Santisimo Nombre del Nino Jesus.

Tenazas, Rosa C. P.
1965 *Santo Niño of Cebu*. Manila: Catholic Trade School.

9 KOREAN GOURD CUPS

Clark, Donald N.
1999 *Guide to Korean Cultural Heritage*. Seoul: Hollym International.
2000 *Culture and Customs of Korea*. Westport, CT: Greenwood.

Han, Suzanne Crowder
1995 *Notes on Things Korean*. Seoul: Hollym Corporation.

Kendall, Laurel
1996 *Getting Married in Korea: Of Gender, Morality, and Modernity*. Berkeley: University of California Press.

Korean Overseas Information Service
1996 *Korean Heritage*. Seoul: Hollym Corporation.

Lee, O-Young
1999 *Things Korean*. Boston: Tuttle.

10 JAPANESE *OBUTSUDAN*

Institute for Japanese Culture and Classics
1988 *Matsuri: Festival and Rite in Japanese Life*. Tokyo: Institute for Japanese Culture and Classics.

Kasahara, Kasuo, Paul McCarthy, and Gaynor Sekimori
2002 *A History of Japanese Religion*. Tokyo: Kosei Publishing.

Kitagawa, Joseph Mitsuo
1987 *On Understanding Japanese Religion*. Princeton: Princeton University Press.

Plutschow, Herbert
1996 *Matsuri: The Festivals of Japan*. Surrey: Japan Library.

Tamura, Yoshiro, and Jeffrey Hunter
2001　*Japanese Buddhism: A Cultural History*. Tokyo: Kosei Publishing.

Tanabe, George J., Jr.
1999　*Religions of Japan in Practice*. Princeton: Princeton University Press.

11 JAPANESE *TAIKO*

De Ferranti, Hugh
2000　*Japanese Musical Instruments*. Oxford: Oxford University Press.

Fromartz, Samuel
1998　"Anything but Quiet: Japanese Americans Reinvent *Taiko* Drumming." *Natural History Magazine* 107 (2): 44–49.

Littleton, C. Scott
2002　*Shinto: Origins, Rituals, Festivals, Spirits, Sacred Places*. Oxford: Oxford University Press.

Malm, William P.
2001　*Traditional Japanese Music and Musical Instruments*. Tokyo: Kodansha International.

Schnell, Scott
1999　*The Rousing Drum: Ritual Practice in a Japanese Community*. Honolulu: University of Hawai'i Press.

12 CHINESE NEW YEAR FOODS

Eberhard, Wolfram
1958　*Chinese Festivals*. London: Abelard-Schuman.

Latsch, Marie-Luise
1984　*Chinese Traditional Festivals*. Beijing: New World Press.

Shui, Amy, and Stuart Thompson
1999　*China*. Food and Festivals Series. Chicago: Raintree Library.

Stepanchuck, Carol, and Charles Wong
1992　*Mooncakes and Hungry Ghosts: Festivals of China*. San Francisco: China Books & Periodicals.
2000　*The Traditional Chinese Festivals and Tales*. Chongqing: Chongqing Publishing.

Yan Liao
2004　*Festivals and Food of China*. Broomall, PA: Mason Crest.

Zhu Oixin
1998　*Traditional Festivals of China*. Paramus, NJ: Homa & Sekey Books.

13–15 COAST SALISH FISH HOOK AND CANOES

Ashwell, Reg
2000　*Coast Salish: Their Art, Culture and Legends*. Seattle: Hancock House.

Carlson, Keith Thor, Jan Perrier, and Xwelixweltel
2001　*A Stlo Coast Salish Historical Atlas*. Seattle: Center for Wooden Boats.

Lincoln, Leslie
1991　*Coast Salish Canoes*. Seattle: Center for Wooden Boats.

Neel, David
1995　*The Great Canoes: Reviving a Northwest Coast Tradition*. Seattle: University of Washington Press.

Suquamish Museum
1985　*The Eyes of Chief Seattle*. Suquamish, WA: The Suquamish Museum.

Wright, Robin K.
1991　*A Time of Gathering: Native Heritage in Washington State*. Seattle: University of Washington Press.

16 NORTHWEST COAST WOLF HEADDRESS

Arima, Eugene, and John Dewhirst
1990　"Nootkans of Vancouver Island," in *Northwest Coast*. Vol. 7 of *Handbook of North American Indians*, 391–411. Washington, DC: Smithsonian Institution.

Black, Martha
1999　*HuupuKwanum Tupaat / Out of the Mist: Treasures of Nuu-chah-nulth Chiefs*. Victoria: Royal British Columbia Museum.

Brown, Steven C., Paul MacCapia, and the Seattle
Art Museum
1998   *Native Visions: Evolution in Northwest Coast Art
        from the Eighteenth through the Twentieth Century.*
        Seattle: University of Washington Press.

Ernst, Alice Henson
1952   *The Wolf Ritual of the Northwest Coast.* Eugene:
        University of Oregon Press.

Inverarity, Robert B.
1967   *Art of the Northwest Coast Indians.* Los Angeles:
        University of California Press.

Shearar, Cheryl
2000   *Understanding Northwest Coast Art: A Guide to
        Crests, Beings, and Symbols.* Seattle: University
        of Washington Press.

Stewart, Hillary
1979   *Looking at Indian Art of the Northwest Coast.*
        Seattle: University of Washington Press.

Wyatt, Gary
1999   *Spirit Faces: Contemporary Masks of the Northwest
        Coast.* Seattle: University of Washington Press.

17 IÑUPIAQ *UMIAQ*

Blackman, Margaret B.
1989   *Sadie Brower Neakok: An Iñupiaq Woman.* Seattle:
        University of Washington Press.

Lipton, Barbara
1977   *Survival: Life and Art of the Alaskan Eskimo.* New-
        ark, NJ: The Newark Museum.

Snaith, Skip, and Tina Rose
1997   *Umiak: An Illustrated Guide.* Eastsound, WA: Wal-
        rose & Hyde.

Spencer, Robert F.
1984   "North Alaska Eskimo: Introduction" and "North
        Alaska Eskimo" in *Arctic.* Vol. 5 of *Handbook of
        North American Indians*, 278–84, 320–37. Washing-
        ton, DC: Smithsonian Institution.

LIST OF CONTRIBUTORS

LARRY ULAAQ AHVAKANA lives and has his studio in Suquamish, Washington. He travels several times a year to his hometown, Barrow, Alaska. He studied fine arts at the Institute of American Indian Art in Santa Fe, New Mexico, and received a Bachelor of Fine Arts from the Rhode Island School of Design. His media include stone, bronze, glass, wood, ivory, and paper. He is most noted for his contemporary figurative work. Many of his images are taken from his Northern Alaska Inupiaq heritage. His work is represented in collections throughout the United States (especially Alaska) and Greenland.

VERONICA LEASIOLAGI BARBER is also known as Talking Chieftess Nofoavaeloloa-o-Lualemagafaigā in her Samoan community. She worked for nineteen years for the Roman Catholic Archdiocese of Seattle as the director for Asian and Pacific Islander affairs and is currently serving a two-year term as the national Samoan consultant for the United States Conference of Catholic Bishops through its Migration and Refugee Services and its Pastoral Care for Migrants and Refugees offices. She holds an MPA degree from Seattle University and is currently the coordinator for the Pacific Northwest regional chapter of the Faleula O Fatua'i'upu, which promotes the teaching of Samoan languages and cultures.

JACK BUZZARD was born in Cebu City, Philippines, and moved to the United States in the early 1950s. He is the son of a U.S. Congressional Medal of Honor recipient. He retired from Northwest Airlines after forty-two years. He is an active member of his church and of the Filipino community of greater Seattle.

MARCELA ANTONIA BUZZARD was born in Cebu City, Philippines. She has lived in the

United States with her husband, Jack, and their family since the early 1960s. She worked for thirty-two years with Teamsters 117 in Seattle.

MAXINE CHAN has resided in the Seattle area for most of her life. She has a passion for the arts and for cuisine, which accounts for her collection of plastic food. To support her art habit, she has been employed in various fields, most recently in social service.

KHAMPHA CHANTHARANGSY was born in Laos. After living in India, where he received his master's degree in sociology, he came to the United States in 1980. He has worked for the Seattle Public Schools for thirteen years, first as an instructional assistant and later as a teacher. Most recently he has been working as a certified interpreter and translator in Lao and Thai and as a citizenship class instructor for the Lao Community Service Office.

RON CHEW is a Chinese American, born and raised in Seattle. He has served as executive director of the Wing Luke Asian Museum in Seattle since 1991.

DONNIE CHIN is director of the International District Emergency Center in Seattle, where he was born and raised (fourth generation).

'IWALANI CHRISTIAN is a *kumu hula* (hula source), a cultural responsibility and position for which she was groomed from a young age on the island of Kaua'i. Her academy of traditional hula practitioners serves as a cultural

caretaker and has been in the Northwest for over thirty years. She dedicates much of her time to cultural education, language studies, and Native Hawaiian issues within the Hawaiian community.

ROSE DANG came to the United States with her husband and five small children in 1976. She is the faculty coordinator of the General Studies and Asian Studies programs at South Seattle Community College and an active leader and board member of numerous Vietnamese American organizations in Seattle.

GEORGE DAVID has traveled worldwide, sharing and teaching not only his art but also his people's culture and history. He serves as a culturalist aboard the *Yorktown Clipper*, a cruise ship that travels the Inside Passage between Seattle and Alaska. His art is well represented in collections in the United States; however, he is currently focusing his efforts on establishing public works in the Seattle area. He recently settled in Neah Bay, Washington.

PEG (KWI-ALQ) DEAM is a Suquamish elder who continues to learn the teachings of her elders. Living on her ancestral land, she loves to work with cedar and wool, creating traditional clothing. Being a lifelong artist, she keeps busy working in many media, but cedar and wool remain her favorites.

LEONARD FORSMAN is trained in archaeology and historic preservation. He is the former director of the Suquamish Tribal Museum and a former Suquamish Tribal Council member. He currently serves as tribal spokesperson for the Suquamish tribe.

DAVID HAWELMAI was born on the island of Eauripik (population 130) in Yap State in the Federated States of Micronesia. After graduating from the Agriculture and Trade School on the island of Pohnpei, he moved to Seattle, where he attended Seattle University. He currently works as a marine machinery mechanic for Puget Sound Naval Shipyard.

VI HILBERT, an elder of the Upper Skagit Tribe, has been honored by Washington State and others for her many years of cultural work. She taught Lushootseed-language courses at the University of Washington before retiring to found and direct Lushootseed Research, which is dedicated to the preservation and perpetuation of the Lushootseed language. She remains active in Native cultural affairs throughout the Northwest.

MOODETTE KA'APANA has resided in Seattle since 1972. She was born and raised in Hawai'i, graduated from Seattle University, and opened her hula school in 1989. She graduated under *uniki* rituals as *kumu hula* in 1994 and was honored to be the instructor of the first hula class offered through the University of Washington Dance Department in the spring of 2004. She continues to perpetuate the art of hula and the beauty of the Hawaiian culture in Seattle.

HELEN KAY, a retired pharmacist, is currently serving as chairperson of the King County Board of Appeals and Equalization. She has been a resident of the Seattle area since the 1960s and has been active on boards of Asian American and King County organizations.

SONIA KIM (SHIN SONG-JA) was born in Korea and came to the United States after receiving her BA in English from Ewha Women's University in Seoul. She has an MSW from the University of Washington and has worked for the past thirty years for the State of Washington in child protective services and currently in interim care. Cofounder of the Korean Community Counseling Center in Seattle, Sonia is also a dream analyst and therapist. Her volunteer work includes hospice care and advisory board positions at the Burke Museum and Seattle Asian Art Museum.

REVEREND DEAN KOYAMA was born and raised in Sacramento, California. He graduated from the Institute of Buddhist Studies with an MA in Buddhist studies. He followed up his graduate work at Ryukoku University in Kyoto, Japan, with an MA in Jodo Shinshu studies. He is an ordained Hompa Hongwanji Jodo Shinshu Buddhist priest and has served the Seattle Betsuin Buddhist Temple (1989–1996) and the Tacoma Buddhist Temple (1996–2002). Currently he is serving as the resident minister for the Mountain View Buddhist Temple in California.

ROKURO (ROCKY) MESIAB was born on Yap in Micronesia. He came to the United States in the late 1970s to attend Lake Superior State University in Michigan and later moved to the Northwest. Rocky was deeply involved in the Micronesian community as a translator and facilitator for island gatherings. Since passing away in 2000, his memory and traditions live on with his two children, Theresa and Kevin, who both continue to reside in the Northwest.

AOTAUMAREWA LORRAINE ELKINGTON MOREHOUSE was born in 1948 and was educated in Wellington, New Zealand. She moved to the United States in 1984. She and her husband, Rick, reside in Port Ludlow, Washington. They have six children.

SAPINA PELE arrived in Seattle as a young child in 1958 and has lived in Seattle ever since. She is married to Reverend Sagato Pele and has five daughters. She has been involved with the Samoan community as an activist since 1973, when she was sent to Philadelphia for training in community involvement in political races. As a former social worker in the Seattle Public Schools, her passion today is keeping public schools public.

SEATTLE MATSURI TAIKO is a youth group sponsored by the Seattle Betsuin Buddhist Temple. The group performs at various festivals throughout the Northwest.

KHAM OUI SIKHANTHAT came to the United States from Laos in 1980. He lives in Seattle and since 1987 has worked for the Seattle Public Schools, first as an instructional assistant and since 1992 as a student and family advocate.

THUY VU received his law degree from the University of Saigon, Vietnam, in 1967 and his doctorate in economics from Michigan State University in 1973. After briefly serving on the faculty of the University of Saigon, he left Vietnam in 1975 as a refugee. He resettled in Olympia, Washington, where he joined the Department of Social and Health Services' Office of Research and Data Analysis. In 1987 he was appointed Washington State coordinator for refugee resettlement. He also serves on the faculty of the University of Washington in the Department of American Ethnic Studies and the Jackson School of International Studies. He is currently the executive director for the Refugee and Immigrant Center in Olympia.

LAURA WONG-WHITEBEAR is the manager of the elders nutrition program for the United Indians of All Tribes Foundation. She is an accomplished weaver and is involved in numerous other Native causes and activities. She is also the founder of the Three Generations Dance Group and the recipient of a 2001 artist fellowship from the National Museum of the American Indian in New York and Washington, DC.

MIRIAM KAHN is a professor of anthropology and chair of the Anthropology Department at the University of Washington. She was the lead curator of "Pacific Voices" and continues to serve as adjunct curator of Pacific ethnology at the Burke Museum in Seattle. She conducted field research in Papua New Guinea in the late '70s and early '80s and in French Polynesia since the early '90s. She has worked at both the American Museum of Natural History in New York and the Field Museum of Natural History in Chicago. She is the author of *Always Hungry, Never Greedy: Food and the Expression of Gender in a Melanesian Society* (Cambridge: Cambridge University Press, 1986) and numerous articles in professional journals. She is currently writing a book on her research in French Polynesia.

ERIN YOUNGER is director of public programs at the Burke Museum in Seattle. She served as project manager of the "Pacific Voices" exhibit, coordinating its development and installation. Her prior work has included arts and heritage program management for King County and Humanities Washington, and serving as curator of Native American art the Heard Museum in Phoenix. She is the coauthor with Victor Masayesva of *Hopi Photographers/Hopi Images* (Tucson: University of Arizona Press, 1983) and author of *Loloma: A Retrospective View* (Phoenix: Heard Museum, 1978), as well as numerous articles on Native American art.

INDEX